SOCIAL STRUCTURE

Social Structure argues for the importance of social structure to analysis within the discipline of sociology. This book provides a thorough introduction to the idea of social structure, laying out the range of difficult issues which arise in analysing social structure. It examines the meanings of the term, the history of its usage within sociology and looks at the more recent developments in thinking on social structure. It sketches a synoptic model for analysing social structures showing how its disparate elements might each be studied using a 'toolkit' of approaches and conceptual resources to analyse particular aspects of social structure.

Charles Crothers is Professor of Sociology at the University of Natal, Durban.

SOCIAL STRUCTURE

Charles Crothers

London and New York

First published 1996
by Routledge
11 New Fetter Lane, London EC4P 4EE

Simultaneously published in the USA and Canada
by Routledge
29 West 35th Street, New York, NY 10001

© 1996 Charles Crothers

Typeset in Garamond by Routledge
Printed and bound in Great Britain by T J Press (Padstow) Ltd,
Padstow, Cornwall

British Library Cataloguing in Publication Data
A catalogue record for this book is available from the
British Library

Library of Congress Cataloguing in Publication Data
Crothers, C.
Social structure / Charles Crothers.
Includes bibliographical references and index.
1. Social structure. 2. Sociology–Methodology. I. Title.
HM131.C845 1996
301'.01–dc20
96–14318 CIP

ISBN 0–415–14946–0

CONTENTS

PREFACE

The concept of Social Structure is important for understanding the brute facts as well as the complexities, subtleties and the bewildering interlinkages and interpenetrations of geographical and time scales which seem to be the mark of current social conditions. The concept refers to descriptions and explanations of people's attributes, attitudes and behaviour in terms of their positions within wider social groupings and, in turn, endeavours to explain the characteristics and dynamics of these collectivities themselves. The metaphor of social structure is powerful yet mystical, and carries with it many overbearing connotations of determinism. This unfortunate aura of the term seems to fit less well in the contemporary intellectual climate, and this lack of congruence has led to some falling away in its use. But it is essential for the developing analytical capacity of Sociology to refurbish the concept and lay out directions in which thinking about social structure should progress.

In the past, thinking about social structures has been channelled within each of several different perspectives which throw light into one or other of its several aspects. These separate treatments need to be brought together, reconciled and interrelated within a wider framework which allows the examination of a wide range of different aspects. This book:

- provides an anchoring statement of the essential questions social structural approaches must tackle;
- lays out the range of difficult issues which arise in analysing social structures;
- examines the meanings of the term and the history of its usage within Sociology;
- sketches a synoptic model for analysing social structures; and
- shows how its disparate elements might each be studied using a toolkit of approaches to analysing particular aspects of social structures.

ACKNOWLEDGMENTS

This book arises from a long-held interest in the central theoretical concepts of sociology and in their application to make sense of real-world social structures, which was instilled in me by my early training at the hands of Allan Levett. It also arises out of the work I have carried out on the theoretical work of Robert K Merton (Crothers 1987) and subsequent work on the Columbia Tradition: reading and talking with various Columbians has been helpful for this project too.

I am thankful, too, for the many others who have encouraged me, or been bemused at my project. But most of the ideas and arguments in this book have arrived from such a multitude of different sources that the task of tracing them would be extremely difficult. The main structures providing me access to library resources as well as the sustenance for writing have been traditional university departments: at the University of Auckland, on leave, and at the University of Kent, Canterbury. Beyond that, more direct help came from only a few sources: David Pearson, Raewyn Peart and Doug Porpora. Justin Leff and Gaynor van Buerden provided long-distance electronic rescue at a difficult point.

It is, of course, somewhat ironic that a book dealing with social structure baulks at analysing the social organisation behind its own delivery. On the other hand, it is a self-exemplification of the approach in the book, which stresses the complexities and sometimes weak effects of social structures.

1

INTRODUCTION
The sociology of social structure

The significance of concepts of social structure, and the extent to which social structural explanations of human behaviour have been invoked, has varied between and within societies, over time and according to circumstances. At some periods, in some societies, human life has been seen as ploughing along pre-set and predictable furrows completely dominated by unchanging and unchallengeable social structures. At other times and places, ideologies of individualism have abounded and the scope and variability of human freedom, creativity and agency have been celebrated. More often, some mix of collective and individual doctrines has been prevalent.

The emphasis given to social structure by sociologists has worked well within the outer bounds set by broader cultural images of social structure. Clearly, there is a continued bias in sociology towards the more socially deterministic approach. After all, for very self-interested academic needs it has usually been held that sociology's goal is to expose the workings of social structures, as opposed to mere patternings of individual psychology. It offers its views of social life in competition with alternative explanations put forward by other social sciences, as well as popular ideologies held by élites and people more generally. Any inability to find at least strong traces of structural determinism therefore constitutes scientific failure. Moreover, many sociologists have been trained to believe that social structures are real, whatever the beliefs held in the culture.

In recent years, after the high-point of 'structuralist' approaches in the late 1960s and 1970s, there has been a faltering in the development of social structural theory and a growing emphasis on human actions, cultural meanings and the significance of bodies in natural environments (cf. Lash and Urry 1984). A result of this trend has been a tendency to ignore or slight the body of social structural explanations which older eras of sociology confidently, even brashly, provided.

More recently again, there seems to be a further revival of interest in social structure in reaction to some of the desolate extremes of postmodernism's denial of social structure. In this book, I attempt to draw together some of the most useful components of the concept which are emerging from recent

1

work and debate. In writing this book, I was able to draw on a growing and often-recent literature, although it proved impossible to include the full range of recent debates. Along with drawing attention to this recent work, this book is concerned to recover and insist on the importance of social structural analysis. Structural analysis is seen as being needed not only to revitalise the confidence of sociology in its ability to provide explanations of the patterning of social life, but is sorely needed as a source of understanding in our trying times.

In this introductory chapter, I will provide a preliminary definition of social structure, followed by an outline. This involves listing the book's goals and limitations, and a discussion of the need for good understanding of social structures in the world at large, particularly within the discipline of Sociology.

WHAT SOCIAL STRUCTURAL ARGUMENTS ARE ABOUT

Social structural explanations are alternatives to, or at least complements of, more frequently employed attributions of social conduct. Very often, when we want to understand some social event or circumstance, we explain this in terms of the particular people involved. For example, we say that we get poor service from the local bureaucracy or store because the people there are horrid or impatient. An alternative ploy is to blame the person-in-charge for not showing the requisite competence or leadership that is required: at least to our eyes. Or if we do present more structural arguments, we are inclined to drum home a particular formula: e.g. that boss must have an impossible job because there are too many people reporting to her, compared to some optimum figure we have extracted from an ancient management text. Because such common views can be easily trotted out, they tend to deflect the application of a more effective structural perspective.

Instead of blaming individuals too readily, as in the above examples, we should check out whether structural arrangements are at fault. People are often more difficult to deal with if they are under pressure, if they are poorly trained or inadequately briefed, if their role involves particularly difficult and conflicting role-expectations, if they are not supplied with adequate resources for carrying out the job, or if they are a subordinate group fighting for better recognition and reward. In other words, the explanation lies with social structural features. This is hardly to say that personalities do not matter. However, even with personality characteristics, people often adapt to social positions rather than the other way around. For example, new counsellors may join an agency with bright challenging views on how to relate to their future clients, but (after some years in the job) may be ground down into much more pragmatic, even punitive, attitudes.

The acid test for a social structural explanation is whether or not changing the actual people involved in a structure is likely to make a difference. If particular types of behaviour are caused by structural arrangements, then changing the personnel is likely to be useless. Because the new personnel will fall into the same structural difficulties, the issue will reappear. It is necessary, rather, to endeavour to change the social structure, although that is a step we too often baulk at.

If structural arguments are used, we should be wary of simplistic formulae. Those who are experienced in a particular area of life may very well have digested some essentials of the way social structures operate best in their experience. However, they may be unaware of the quite limited circumstances under which their experience-based rules-of-thumb hold true. A general lesson that many sociologists have learned is that there are varieties of social structure, and that we must be attuned to the different social circumstances under which different structural arrangements are appropriate. There are no easy golden rules about how to set up effective or just social structures.

On the whole, people are probably more likely to 'psychologise' than to be overly-deterministic in their explanations of social life. On the other hand, once they get into the swing of it, overly-deterministic structural arguments can be promiscuously thrown around. Structures can be blamed for things and attributed far more causal agency than they deserve: almost as if they were uninhabited by ordinary, responsible and energetic people.

Structural analyses must avoid falling into either extreme. Developing sensitive structural analyses can be difficult, but they have an important role to play in the repertoire of social explanations.

A PRELIMINARY VIEW OF SOCIAL STRUCTURE

What, then, is this strange animal that is being referred to? In this section, I provide two definitions to open the discussion and then sketch a very brief overview of the approach to social structure which the book will then develop in more depth. This brief overview is a guide to what is to be expanded on in more detail throughout subsequent chapters.

But first, a word on a terminological point. Along with other writers on social structure, I have found difficulty in finding a generic term to refer to different sorts of social entities without importing any particular commitments to particular features. In particular, a term which spans the difference between 'social categories' or 'heaps' of socially unattached people with some similarities, compared to social solidarities which are intensively interconnected, would be valuable. Runciman's neologism to handle this particular issue is 'systac', which he defines in a generic fashion as 'A group or category of persons in specified roles ... when ... the persons have, by virtue of their roles, a distinguishable and more than transiently similar location, and on that account, a common interest. . . . ' (1989: 20); e.g. castes, classes, élites or women as a category/grouping. However, this term is used particularly at a societal level of analysis. I will use 'social grouping' as a general-purpose term, hopefully stripped of some of the unfortunate trappings of surplus meaning such terms invariably attract. Where the environment of a social grouping is spoken of, often (and more generally) the society, this will be referred to as 'the wider social order'.

In general, social structure refers to the relations (especially more permanent, stable relationships) among people, between groupings or institutions, and backwards and forwards between people and groupings. Social structure is a descriptive and explanatory concept which is used to show how the social behaviour, attitudes, attributes and trajectories of individuals (and the social groupings they are involved in) are shaped, and why there are various patterns of allocation of resources and rewards. It is the key thrust of the argument that what someone does/has/is/believes etc. is shaped by their position in the social structure. In turn, the patternings of social structure itself are explained by a variety of both external and internal factors. Human action in turn, feeds back to affect the operation of social structures: there is an ongoing, reciprocal process of shaping and feedback between participants and social structures.

More technically, this definition can be spelled out to suggest that social structure refers to the ways in which social groupings (which may be more or less organised) are involved:

- through strategies, tactics and less conscious action;
- in drawing on and creating ideologies, resources and contacts;
- to maintain and/or change themselves within the broader social order.

This definition only indicates the parameters of many possibilities of different arrangements among its three components. It allows for a wide range of variation among social structures, such as that:

- social groupings may vary considerably in composition (including the possibility of groupings composed of quite unconnected separate individuals);
- their activities may vary considerably in terms of degree of conscious direction and decision-making;
- their aims may range over a wide span of 'goals' (e.g. aggressive change, desperate defence, resigned defeat etc.); and
- their relationships within their setting(s) may also differ markedly (e.g. a social grouping may usually be locked into some form of relationship with others, but not under all circumstances).

This definition draws attention to similarities among all social structures, but it also points to the ways social structures differ along a range of different axes.

4

GOALS OF BOOK

Nearly half a century ago, Robert Merton published his review of social structural theory (1949). This was an early and highly influential sifting of views on how sociology might cumulatively build up an understanding of social structures. A decade later, Nadel (1957) began to develop a focused and rigorous approach to studying social structure. Another two decades on, twenty years before the present, Peter Blau (1975) organised reviews of social structural theorising in the 1960s and 1970s. The concept has been periodically but partially reviewed since then. However, no single source handles the task with sufficient breadth and depth. This book attempts to systematically report on progress over the last half-century, since Merton's volume was published.

The aim is not so much to advance new solutions for old riddles, as to at least clarify the various issues involved in analysing social structures. The book also endeavours to lay a foundation for further work. Above all, I hope to communicate vivid illustrations of the power of social structural analysis. In order to keep the huge range of material under control, abject simplification is often resorted to, with guidance being given to reading for further exploration.

The particular aims of this book are:

- to urge the focusing of sociology on a core of central concepts;
- to draw attention to the concept of social structure and to reinforce its importance as a sociological conceptual tool;
- to lay out various conceptual tools needed to conduct an analysis of a social structure, and to indicate something of the skills needed to wield them;
- to make some observations on the peculiar character of 'social structure' as a sociological concept and term;
- to (re)assemble the set of theoretical issues to which structural analysis must attend;
- to trace the trajectory of work on social structure, and to array the types of conceptualisation of it that have been displayed in sociology;
- to draw attention to more recent developments in thinking on social structure which are largely ignored in standard graduate school curricula;
- to argue that to examine social structure requires the meshing together of a range of approaches, drawn from what is in effect a toolkit of concepts for studying social structures.

The way the book is written backs up the tasks it attempts to achieve. Sociology should not just pass on what is already known. It should seek to encourage the expansion of sociological knowledge. To enable this, this book seeks to teach something of the craft of actually carrying out social analyses. Sociology is presented as a discipline providing the ready-to-hand tools which facilitate the analysis of social structures. The book intends to be practical and scholarly: as

5

well as providing a stock-taking of what we know about social structures in general, to lay out the conceptual resources needed to develop analyses of particular social structures.

How these goals for this book are to be achieved is overviewed in the next two sections.

ORGANISATION OF THE ARGUMENT AND BOOK

The main argument of the book is presented after the necessary prior tasks of reviewing different conceptualisations of social structure (Chapter 2) and reviewing the history of modern theories of social structure (Chapter 3).

The main argument of this book then proceeds in two steps: one dealing with the *nature* of social structure (Chapter 4) and the other with the *scope* of social structures (Chapter 5). The first of these two substantive chapters examines what appear to be some of the key desiderata for any analysis of social structure. Any adequate account of the nature of social structures must grapple with issues such as the relation between structure and agency, between macro- and micro-level viewpoints, and how to allow for the interplay between culture and social structure etc.

The second step of the main argument then pulls together a range of different visions of social structure. As opposed to the unabashedly theoretical nature of Chapter 4, Chapter 5 has a more pragmatic, eclectic interest in merging the useful viewpoints which more delimited approaches can offer. The approaches to social structure which need to be included in any comprehensive account are, I believe, those in the following check-list:

- classical status-and-role theory;
- network analyses;
- accounts of collective social actors;
- depictions of 'fields' or institutional areas;
- social constructionist accounts of the building and maintenance of social structures;
- distributional accounts of allocations of people and resources within social structures;
- structural change analyses;
- life-course and life-event analyses; and
- spatial and temporal aspects of social structures.

On the face of it, there are major difficulties in working each of these rather different perspectives into a common framework, since several claim to be explicitly opposed to others, and several rather different root metaphors are drawn upon. However, I will argue that the aspects of social structure analysis I take from each of these frameworks shares a common core understanding, and that much of the incompatibility between these various perspectives arises at a meta-theoretical level, which does not necessarily infect the more useful aspects of each of the conceptual tools that have been developed. Assembling and then relating these frameworks is the main task of this book.

TOWARDS A 'NATURAL SCIENCE' OF SOCIAL STRUCTURE?

Any approach to understanding social structure is set within a particular way of studying society. The particular vision one has of social structure will be largely pre-determined by one's view of sociology as a whole and how sociological studies should be conducted.

The way the book is written also reflects a stance on how sociology should be approached. Accordingly, I will endeavour to briefly indicate my approach to sociology as a 'discipline'. However, since this is not a treatise in the philosophy of social science, the treatment will be brief. Similar issues are raised again in Chapter 4.

Hobbes suggested that anything that was not scientific should be consigned to the flames. This view is too strongly put! However, the idea that sociology should be concerned to advance scientific laws runs along this line of thought. Such a 'positivist' view of sociology is now less frequent. An alternative view of sociology as being concerned with the in-depth investigation of a few cases is increasingly being advanced. However, in this book an intermediate approach is advanced, in which there is seen to be a dialectical interplay between the stock of concepts held by a discipline and the confusions of the real world.

It does seem that sociology can only advance its knowledge-base if both its theoretical and empirical work is directly related to ongoing issues about the operation of social structures. Unless a study adds generally or specifically to our knowledge of the operation of social structures, it may be of more limited sociological value.

Related to this, sociologists ought to be able to mobilise the relevant portions of their available stock of knowledge in relation to particular circumstances. A central aspect of this is that they should be well-drilled in the tasks of analysing particular social structures, or groupings of social structural units. An analysis should provide a theoretically-based account of the key features of a particular social structural unit and how the unit operates. While an analysis might well lead to the collection of empirical research, and often it is based on pre-existing research data, it may be possible to construct analyses with only a quite thin set of information. The point of analyses is that, although they relate to particular empirically-occurring structures, they need not be fully empirically tested. Analyses mediate between the accumulated stock of knowledge and detailed information about particular cases.

In short, we should keep on methodically building a systematic understanding of how and why social structures work, while pushing out further and further our stock of empirical examples. Particular analyses and the stock of conceptual tools should mutually interact to the advantage of each.

An unfortunate connotation of a toolkit approach is that it can be taken to advocate an eclectic and undisciplined falling-to with any tool which comes to hand. The preferred image is, rather, that of a well-ordered workshop in which clearly labelled tools are carefully displayed and applied only where appropriate, according to a theoretically-based workshop manual.

Although attention has been directed to the building of theories rather than case-orientated analyses, something approximating the approach I am advocating was developed in the 1960s. Theorising in sociology was seen as an activity as much as theory is a product. It is important to consider the skills needed for theory-building, as well as the general approaches which can be used. Stinchcombe has argued that 'Theory ought to create the capacity to invent explanations' (1968: 3). He laid out a specific challenge of what is required to master the craft of sociology when he suggested that

> . . . the model of social theorising as a practical scientific activity ought to be an ability to carry out the following task within an hour or two.
>
> Choose any relation between two or more variables which you are interested in; invent at least three theories, not now known to be false, which might explain these relations; choosing appropriate indicators, derive at least three different empirical consequences from each theory, such that factual consequences distinguish among the theories.
>
> (Stinchcombe 1968: 13)

If the carrying out of one's own structural analysis is thought to be too difficult a goal, an easier goal would be that the reader of this book will be in a better position to be a more careful and critical reader of others' structural analyses: i.e. a better client.

However, I differ somewhat from what Stinchcombe (1968) and other members of the 1960s school of 'theory-constructionists' taught. They argued for a catch-as-catch-can approach to developing theories. Their books emphasised the form (or the how-to) of theory-building at the cost of being relatively unconcerned about the content of these theories. However, the stock of knowledge about social structures is already far too replete for such a cavalier approach to content, and our studies of social structure must be much more disciplined by drawing on readily available material. Nevertheless, I strongly endorse the theory-constructionists' emphasis on creativity and on developing explicit theoretical models.

LIMITATIONS OF THE COVERAGE IN THIS BOOK

There are several points on which the boundaries and limitations of this book should be more clearly outlined.

Theory and methodology

In keeping with its purpose of enabling structural analyses, this book briefly refers to some aspects of the methodological discussions that feature in many of the more recent approaches to social structure. There are advantages in this, as methodologists have often identified some of the more crucial issues which need to be addressed in understanding social structures. Working out the conceptual difficulties and developing the strategies needed to study something is a useful discipline in developing important conceptualisations. However, this book does not stray far into such methodological matters. Indeed, where at all possible, I am concerned with extracting theoretical ideas from the thickets of methodological discussions.

In terms of social research methods that are relevant to studying social structure, the full gamut can be appropriately pressed into service as suits the occasion. Where possible, a 'triangulation' in approach is important, with quantitative, qualitative and historical and structural data all being relevant. However, the point of social structural analysis is (as suggested above) to provide a framework of interpretation on which social research methods and their resulting data can be hung.

Culture, social structure and personality

The emphasis on social structure is not intended to deny the causal efficacy of alternative approaches, such as those stressing culture or personality. It is not intended, even, to argue the pre-eminence of social structural approaches compared to others, although it is my suspicion that this is indeed the most useful route towards more effective social explanations! All are needed and are complementary to each other. However, the enormous complexity of the social order creates massive difficulties for those who would study it. It is important to try to maintain the integrity of each particular form of analysis and learn to carry out each effectively, without becoming too diverted by complexities. Once a particular type of explanation has been confidently developed, it should become a firmer framework on to which to attach complementary explanations.

The macro- and micro-levels

Sometimes a distinction is drawn between the micro-level 'interactional order' (in which people face each other in sequences of social situations) and the broader web of enduring and larger-scale relationships which bind social entities together. This distinction is itself problematic (see Mouzelis 1990 for further discussion on this point). Even quite fleeting social encounters are shaped by social structural forms and give rise to social structure. However, these types of situations are considered here at best only fleetingly, and attention is focused on rather more institutionalised and durable social patterns.

Ethno-centrism

This book is almost entirely set within the 'sociological present' and within the 'Western cultural world'. Indeed, a major limit is that it draws almost entirely on English language sources. A variety of major recent theorists whose work impinges on the understanding of social structure are not treated. While a sociology much more attuned to the variety of social structures across time, space and social conditions would be especially valuable, it might differ only slightly from the present rendition. It seems to me that, at least in principle, the conceptual tools for analysing social structure will be generally common across cultural worlds, although the particular forms of social structures within them may vary considerably. On the other hand, exposure to wider views will undoubtedly fine-tune our more general conceptions, and lead to some exciting additions.

More specific forms of social structure

Some areas of sociology are particularly pertinent for understanding social structure. Such fields are those where issues of structure arise most fervently and are at the forefront in the development of deeper conceptualisations.

Those specialist areas of particular importance for advancing social structural analysis have changed from time to time, but certainly include social class analysis, which is widely still taken to be the paradigmatic area for understanding social structure. Alongside class analysis are arrayed feminist theory and theory relating to race and ethnicity. Indeed, a useful 'operational definition' of social structure can be the investigation of the operation of class, gender and ethnic structural dimensions within societies. (The collection by Wright 1989 raises broader questions about the nature of class as one major face of social structure.) In each of these areas, issues of social structure have been incisively debated and more general treatments have much to learn from these more specific renditions. On the other hand, it is obsolete to reduce social structural analysis to class analysis, or even the more recent triptych of class–gender–ethnicity.

Another area of Sociology which is often pertinent in discussions of social structure is that pertaining to 'deviance', due to its central concern with the different social causation and reaction to 'normal' and 'deviant' conduct, which is at the heart of social life. Several theorists (e.g. Touraine, see Scott 1991) have also pointed to 'social movements' as containing the seeds of social futures and also revealing the levers of social change, and therefore of considerable interest to sociologists, beyond this particular topic of study itself.

Particular content areas of sociology can also be of considerable pertinence.

Given that much social activity is fundamentally shaped by the materialist foundation of social life, particular importance is accorded to the sociology of economic phenomena (see Block 1990; Granovetter and Swedberg 1992). Certainly, sociologies which encompass only the 'non-economic residue' of social life often seem flaccid in terms of the explanations they are able to provide. However, despite what many might think of as quite the 'opposite' area of social life, cultural sociology requires just as much attention to the social forms in which the production and reception of cultural commodities are contained.

It would be a tall order to provide anything like a reasonably balanced account of the different types of social structure or of the lessons to be garnered from each of the various fields of sociology. This book makes no systematic attempt to do so. Although I recognise the importance of drawing on a wide array of areas of sociology, these are only raided to illustrate general points.

Other disciplines' views of social structure

Similarly, debates about various aspects of social structure have arisen in each social science discipline. For example, theoretical discussions on 'power' will often see this as strongly linked with social structure. Such conceptual links have taken a variety of forms. In this book, attention is focused only on those debates that have arisen within mainstream sociology, and which clearly use the term 'social structure'. While some material from other disciplines and approaches is occasionally used, little attempt has been made to achieve reasonable coverage of important debates such as those pertaining to the nature of power, or of the relevance of particular concepts of social structure in relation to women or to particular ethnic groups.

THE RETURN TO SOCIAL STRUCTURE

Societal needs for structural explanation

In the opening paragraphs I noted that social structure is a concept whose importance varies. I would now like to expand a little on the relevance of a revamped conception of social structure, firstly for general social debates, and then more narrowly for sociology itself.

Skocpol nicely presses this point:

> Ours is an era when no existing macrosociological theory seems adequate, yet when the need for valid knowledge of social structures and transformations has never been greater.
>
> (1984: 385)

There clearly is a social need for a 'return to the social'. Not only is better social analysis needed to help retrieve many countries and other social groupings from recent difficulties and to face mounting current problems, but much effort is still needed to recast sociological advice and to project it forward into helping shape the social forms of the future.

A central conceptual role for sociology

As well as societal needs for sociological knowledge, a refurbished sociological understanding of social structure would be helpful for the discipline itself.

It is difficult to provide a definition of Sociology without drawing on a concept of social structure. Almost all definitions of sociology imply 'social structure': the study of social relations, interaction, groups etc. It is clearly one of the few important concepts in the discipline. It is even arguable, as this book attempts to show, that some of the array of other central sociological terms are merely subconcepts within a broader social structure framework. Evidence from textbook coverage and occasional forays into investigating those concepts held as important by sociologists back this up (see the survey results cited in Cole 1979).

Hechter, although a virulent rational choice theorist, has nevertheless ringingly proclaimed this point:

> These days – perhaps more than ever – sociologists disagree about many things, but one thing about which nearly all can agree is that social structures constitute the discipline's keystone. The explanation of the genesis of these emergent-level phenomena has always been a central sociological concern.
>
> (Hechter, in Huber 1991: 46)

A related argument is that, if sociologists do not openly continue to develop and propagate theories of social structure, ideas pushed by other groups will rush in to fill the vacuum. Sociologists have to be ready with adequate social structural analyses to clearly point to the importance of these often-neglected aspects of society.

Moreover, beyond the usefulness of refocusing more sociological effort around the concept of social structure, there remains the sheer intrinsic excitement of exploring the complex intellectual issues involved. Abrams' statement of the intellectual challenges of sociology conveys this excitement:

> The paradox of human agency is hardly a new discovery. . . . The problem of agency is the problem of finding a way of accounting for human experience which recognises simultaneously and in equal measure that history and society are made by constant and more or less purposeful individual action and that individual action, however purposeful, is made by history and society. How do we, as active subjects make a world of objects which then, as it were, become subjects making us their

objects? It is the problem of individual and society, consciousness and being, action and structure. . . .

(Abrams 1982: xiii)

CONCLUSION

In this opening chapter I have sketched in something of the demand for explanations in terms of social structures and then indicated the broad shape of how I intend to show how sociological concepts of social structure might supply this need. I have also pointed out that terms such as 'social structure' are developed and used within social contexts.

The parameters of this book have been set out in this chapter, and its rationale presented. In Chapter 2, I review some of the meanings associated with social structure in the course of examining three layers of usages. This is then complemented in Chapter 3 by a historical review, which allows sketches of several important theories of social structure to be given and criticisms of them rehearsed. Chapters 4 and 5 provide the main argument: first, about the nature of social reality and then about the conceptual tools needed to examine its scope.

As Table 1.1 illustrates, this book's attempts to provide a conceptual tool-kit (mainly in Chapter 5, but also drawing on Chapter 4), which will help in the development of structural analyses of concrete 'social reality' (as illustrated in Chapter 2). The deeper theorectical issues underlying this 'took-kit' are discussed in Chapter 4, and the overall approach outlined in Chapter 6 (also drawing on Chapter 1).

Table 1.1 Levels of analysis used in book and appropriate chapters

'Social reality'	⟷	Structural analyses	⟷	Conceptual tool-kit	⟷	Deeper theoretical issues	⟷	Approaches to sociology
		Chapter 2		Chapter 5 (and 3)		Chapter 4		Chapter 6 (and 1)

2

USES OF THE TERM
'SOCIAL STRUCTURE'

In this chapter, I explore the meanings accorded the term 'social structure'. This task begins with a selective review of official definitions and then moves to a broad-ranging examination of the field of meanings within which this term sits. The chapter then moves on to examine various uses to which the term 'social structure' is sometimes put. As it is soon found that a direct assault to yield the meaning of the concept is not very successful, a more circuitous path is needed. Accordingly, the second half of the chapter is a presentation of a range of illustrative examples, from which implicit meanings of the term can be gleaned. This range of examples has a further purpose of providing more concrete material which can be drawn on in the remainder of the book. Even more importantly, these examples exhibit something of the power and excitement which interesting structural analyses can provide.

OFFICIAL DEFINITIONS

Dictionary definitions

According to the Oxford English Dictionary, de Tocqueville was the first to use the term 'social structure' when he argued in 1835 that 'the Constitution of the United States ... consists of two distinct social structures, connected ... and encased one within the other'. Its next reference is to Spencer followed by references in the 1940s (Fortes) and 1960s (Lévi-Strauss). It seems strange that OED did not find the intervening 70 years rather more heavily populated by usages of the term.

More specialist sociological dictionaries provided the following:

> Though one of the most frequent terms in sociology, this has no specific and universally accepted meaning. . . . A pattern of social interdependence showing continuity over time (patterns which change more slowly than the particular personnel who constitute them).
>
> (Mennell 1983: 367)

Structure may be defined as an organised body of mutually connected parts. In social structure the parts are relationships among persons and the organised body of parts may be considered to be coincident with the society as a whole.

(Heer 1992: 613)

Eister provides the longest definition:

In the sense in which Spencer and many more recent sociologists have used the concept, social structure refers to a more or less distinctive arrangement (of which there may be more than one type) of specialised and mutually dependent institutions (and the institutional organisations of positions and/or of actors which they imply) all evolved in the natural course of events as groups of human beings, with given needs and capacities, have interacted with each other (in various modes of interaction) and sought to cope with their environment.

(Eister 1964: 668)

This extended definition is contrasted with a formal view in which 'social structure is seen as consisting of (a) an arrangement of positions or statuses variously created and maintained, and/or (b) a network of relationships among persons or actors' (Eister 1964: 668).

In the course of his review of types of social structural theory, Blau provides a rather different (ostensive) type of definition which points to the wide array of phenomena that may be involved:

Many different approaches have developed to improve our understanding of social structures and their dynamics. They center attention on a great variety of subjects including the class structure and its significance for historical developments; the evolutionary process of increasing differentiation in social structures; the dialectical process of structural change; the division of labour with its consequences for interdependence and conflict; the forms of associations that structure social relations; the structural-functional analysis of institutional subsystems; the status-sets and role-sets that clarify the dynamics of social structures; the structural roots of deviance and rebellion; the interrelations between environment, population and social structure; the construction of social reality; the structural analysis of kinship and myths.

(Blau 1975: 2)

Blau's definition gives a good handle on what is often meant by the term, and certainly this approach is more meaty than the dictionary definitions.

15

Our masters' voices

There are several collections of sociological terms or quotations (e.g. Sills and Merton 1991), but these yielded only limited material, so it is necessary to search out for definitions provided by important sociological authors. These definitions are now presented more or less chronologically in order that the flavour of the historical development of the concept might be sampled:

> ... a social system consists in a plurality of individual actors interacting with each other in a situation which has at least a physical or environmental aspect, actors who are motivated in terms of a tendency to the 'optimisation of gratification' and whose relation to their situations, including each other, is identified and mediated in terms of a system of culturally structured and shared symbols.
>
> (Parsons and Shils 1951)

Merton defines social structure (in contrast to culture) as 'that organised set of social relationships in which members of the society or group are variously implicated' (1968 [1949]: 216).

Firth states:

> Social structure may include critical or basic relationships arising similarly from a class system based on relations with the soil. Other aspects of social structure arise through membership in other kinds of persistent groups, such as clans, castes, age-sets, or secret societies. Other basic relations again are due to position in a kinship system. . . .
>
> (Firth 1951: 32)

Nadel sums up his view as 'We arrive at the structure of a society through abstracting from the concrete population and its behaviour the pattern or network (or 'system') of relationships obtaining "between actors in their capacity of playing roles relative to one another" ' (1957: 12).

Udy points out that: 'The concept "social structure" is, paradoxically, so fundamental to social science as to render its uncontested definition virtually impossible', which he attributes to the primordial quality of any basic concept (1968: 489). He then goes on to provide the definition ' . . . the totality of patterns of collective human phenomena that cannot be explained solely on the basis of human heredity and/or the non-human environment'.

Finally, Giddens might be seen as representing more recent social theorists: 'Structure . . . refers, in social analysis, to the structuring properties allowing the "binding" of time–space in social systems, the properties which make it possible for discernibly similar social practises to exist across varying spans of time and space and which lend them "systemic" form' (1984: 17).

As this round-up clearly shows, much more space is needed to develop a useful understanding.

HISTORY OF THE TERMS

Since such short and formal definitions do not uncover various of the layers of the term's meaning, a better route might be through a historical tracing of meanings. Sewell cites Foucault to suggest that structure is a general metaphor and that 'such usages originated... in 17th and 18th century botany, from which they spread to other natural and social sciences' (1992: 2).

However, Williams in his *Keywords* provides a rather more lengthy account of the linguistic history of the term 'structure'. The earliest usages in the fifteenth century referred to the process of building. By the seventeenth century it referred both to the whole product and the manner of construction – the latter being the fount of more modern usages. In particular, the latter emphasised the inner structure: the arrangements among constituent parts. In this century, too, the term was used in anatomy as a contrast to the functioning (or performance) of a body part. In the 1870s, usages contrasted internal arrangements and (surface) decoration. In the twentieth century in linguistics, and then other social sciences, structure signalled the analytical study of languages rather than a comparative/historical approach (which had been quite appropriate for the study of more familiar European languages).

> Structure was preferred to process because it emphasised a particular and complex organisation of relations, often at very deep levels. But what were being studied were nevertheless living processes, whereas structure, characteristically, from its uses in building and engineering, and in anatomy, physiology and biology, expressed something fairly fixed and permanent, even hard.
>
> (Williams 1983: 303)

Williams points to similar complexities in the meanings of related terms such as form and system. He also draws a distinction between orthodox structuralism and genetic structuralism, with the former involving permanent constitutive human formations, whereas the latter 'still emphasises deep constitutive formations of a structural kind, but which sees these as being built up and broken down at different stages in history' (1983: 305). In other words, the latter emphasises 'conditions' whereas the former concentrates on universals.

Finally, Williams addresses a particularly important distinction:

> It is a very fine point, in description of any system or structure, whether emphasis is put on the relations between people and between people and things, or on the relationships which include the relations and the people and the things related. It is clear from the history of structure and structural that the words can be used with this emphasis: to include the actual construction with special reference to its mode of construction; or

17

to isolate the mode of construction in such a way as to exclude both ends of the process – the producers (who have intentions related to the mode chosen, as well as experience from the material being worked) and the product. . . .

(Williams 1983: 305–6)

He also notes that 'much structuralist analysis is formalist in the sense of separating form and content and giving form priority' (1983: 306).

Another important differentiation, which Williams does not note, is the one between structure as the relationships among units, and the somewhat wider vision of structure as including patterned characteristics among the units, irrespective of any ties between them.

SYNONYMS AND ANTONYMS

Again, this historical tracing provides useful insights, but is not specifically tied to the concept of social structure. It would clearly be useful to attempt to pull the various threads together into an overall map of the ranges of possible meanings.

The meaning of any term is located within what are often multi-layered and overlapping fields of meanings, since the meaning of any one concept is derived from various contrasts and similarities. With 'social structure' as a double-term, there are extra difficulties as attention has to be paid to both parts of the pair – 'social' and 'structure' – as well as the combination.

There is a range of fairly straightforward synonyms: social . . . order, arrangement, composition, fabric, form, organisation, pattern, system, web etc. On the whole, these can be used as broad synonyms. 'Social order' may imply rather more consensus than other terms, and 'social system' may imply a more definite closed system of interactive interrelationships. 'Society' can have a rather more differentiated meaning since it is often used to refer to that particular form of social structure which is largely self-sufficient and self-contained (e.g. tribes or nation-states).

It is interesting that whereas the 'structure' element of the pair has numerous synonyms, the 'social' part seems far less likely to vary. Sometimes, though, the social is incorporated within a wider, portmanteau term (e.g. socio-cultural or socio-economic). And, of course, social is bedevilled with the double-meaning of 'friendliness' or social activity, as well as its possible extension to socialist.

The range of possible meanings should not be exaggerated. Although both synonyms and antonyms appear to stretch off into the distance, a listing of frequently used paired opposites can be arrayed alongside each other, as laid out in Table 2.1. The various meanings often involved with 'social structure' are included in the left-hand column while antonyms are arrayed alongside them in the right-hand column.

The reason for drawing together this array of terms is that it conveys the range of possibilities out of which any particular conception of social structure is likely to be constructed. It is a smorgasbord menu from which particular combinations might be taken. This set of paired terms and counter-terms is the residue from the whole history of attempts to deploy the term 'social structure' from various viewpoints. The meanings of most of these particular terms are further pursued in Chapter 4.

Table 2.1 Antinomies of social structure

Synonyms	Antonyms
structure	anti-structure
order	chaos
static: permanence	process: change
uniform	contingent
determinism	free will
form	content
collective	individual
methodological collectivism	methodological individualism
cross-sectional: presentist	historical
objective	subjective
patterns of attributes of units	relationships among units
social: determinist	cultural: meaningful
macro-level	micro-level

It seems difficult to clearly order the various pairs in terms of any obvious criteria. However, in general, I have endeavoured to place more abstract differentiations higher on the listing, and more specific ones lower down. The first few pairs in Table 2.1 are the most general: the remainder represent various dimensions of meaning along which any use of the term structure may be placed.

Sometimes, a particular distinction may not be salient to a definition of social structure. And some combinations may draw terms from either column: for example, 'cultural structure' may be analysed from a deterministic stance rather than as being seen as organised solely in terms of internal meaning. Moreover, the contrasts in the various rows of the table have been portrayed in starkly binary terms: in practice, analytical work in sociology must inevitably work in terms of more subtle differentiations along each of the various of these dimensions. While the binary oppositions of the table crudely lay out the boundaries of the conceptual dimensions, the social structure analyst's important task is to find the best ways of reworking these dualisms into more subtly-hewn concepts.

The remainder of this book endeavours to work within the agenda set up by this table in order to gradually provide more subtle distinctions.

SOCIAL USAGES OF THE TERM

Words can also be weapons. The term 'social structure' can be pressed into service to support various interests. As we shall see, sometimes these interests are served by not making the concept too clear, even if this does not assist ease of communication! Indeed, some interests may continually undermine attempts at greater clarity, and it is useful to be aware of this.

Social structure as a boundary-marker for sociology

In the attempt by university-based disciplines to each carve out their own distinctive niche, it is not surprising that appropriate vocabularies have been advanced to support this.

Claims over the same or similar phenomena are made, using different terms, by different disciplines. In endeavouring to create a boundary with anthropology, sociology has sometimes used its preference for social structure over the term culture favoured by anthropologists. Indeed, the attention to some matters within anthropology is often termed a 'sociological' approach. National traditions in social science disciplines have also been marked off by different usages, so that 'American cultural anthropology' has been contrasted with 'British social anthropology'. American anthropologist, Raymond Murphy, has commented interestingly on this point:

> The British penchant for the word 'social' and the centrality of the concept of 'culture' in American anthropology are not significant differentiators when one considers how diversely each is used in actual analyses. Even more important is the fact that in most monographs the words could be totally omitted without changing the perspective or results. Culture and social structure are used in exactly the same way and to refer to the same things by their respective champions. This has been recognised by Fortes . . . who said that social anthropologists study what others call 'culture' but from the perspective of social structure. . . . What each has done has been to practise an imperialism of words, placing the total subject matter under one rubric or the other, and thereby destroying the differentiating and analytical functions of terminology. . . .
>
> (Murphy 1972: 16)

Surely, too much concern with disciplinary markers is a trap?

Social structure as an 'absent term'

However, a more usual pattern of use of the term is quite the opposite. Gallie (1955–56) – among a plethora of other commentators – has drawn attention to the complexities of sociological discussions by pointing out that many sociological terms are 'contested'. While a range of people may share the use of a term, the meanings behind the term may diverge radically. Different usages of the term may be each embedded within quite incommensurate paradigms. Therefore, conflict is likely to arise over the meanings to be accorded the more important of such terms within the sociological lexicon.

However, at least within sociology, social structure is seldom a 'contested concept'. Rather, it is an 'absent concept'. While the term is frequently paraded by sociological writers, it is infrequently backed up with a definition, let alone a more in-depth theoretical discussion.

Books with 'social structure' emblazoned on their covers more often than not fail to deliver on the implicit promise that the concept will be thoroughly deployed. Indexes of sociology books often do not list the term, or at best indicate only fleeting references. (This is prevalent even among books with 'social structure' in their title!)

The importance of the term is signalled by its widespread use. Yet this widespread usage seems accompanied with a reluctance to specify its content. It is not clear why the concept is not elaborated. Perhaps, it is considered too obvious to need any further attention. Perhaps the term is thought to evoke enough meaning on its own to not need the distraction of further definition. It seems often to be used as a synonym for 'sociological analysis' more generally.

Blau, introducing his book of commissioned essays on this very topic, provides further and undoubtedly the definitive proof of these difficulties sociologists seem to have with the term 'social structure'. In commenting on the writers of the essays in his collection he says:

> . . . the main idea in their conceptualisation of social structure [must] be inferred, because some do not explicitly define the concept, and some that do then reveal in their discussion that the terse definition fails to capture the meaning social structure seems to have for them. Most sociologists' concept of social structure is rich with connotations and implications, to which a single definition cannot easily, if at all, do justice. This is undoubtedly the reason that many choose to abstain from supplying a definition of the concept.
>
> (Blau 1975:10)

The power and the mystery: connotations of the term

More recently, Sewell goes on to explain this abstinence of definition by nicely portraying some of the subtleties behind its usage:

The term structure empowers what it designates. Structure in its nominative sense, always implies structure in its transitive verbal sense. Whatever aspect of social life we designate as structure is posited as 'structuring' some other aspect of social existence . . . . Structure operates in social scientific discourse as a powerful metonymic device, identifying some part of a complex social reality as explaining the whole. It is a word to conjure with in the social sciences. In fact, structure is less a precise concept than a kind of founding or epistemic metaphor of social scientific – and scientific – discourse. For this reason, no formal definition can succeed in fixing the term's meaning: the metaphor of structure continues its essential if somewhat mysterious work in the constitution of social scientific knowledge despite theorists' efforts at definition.

(Sewell 1992: 2)

How a concept is received will depend on its fit with the cultural ambience of the times. Sewell goes on to point out the difficulties engendered in contemporary times by some of the common usages of social structure: the term's connotations imply a vision of social structure which is too hard and reified, too impervious to change and too contradictory, especially in terms of the ranges of subject-matter it implies. This misfit between the tone of the concept and current sensibilities may account for a decline in its use.

IMPLICIT USES OF SOCIAL STRUCTURE: EXAMPLES OF STRUCTURAL ANALYSES

If sociologists have been poor in providing general images of social structure, they certainly have not failed in providing numerous insightful analyses. The general points about social structure to be made in this book can be both anticipated and made more vivid by several acute illustrations. (See Perrow 1970, chapter 1, for a particularly vigorous exposition of the sociological viewpoint in general terms.) Contemplation on these examples will assist further in the more immediate quest of this chapter, which is to explore the term's meanings in use.

There are countless examples of good social structural analyses: these few are among many which I have found exciting. Others of course will have their own favourites. The listing is organised in order from smaller-scale social settings up to larger ones.

Humour

Rose Coser (1960) was able to show how such an apparently trivial area of social life as humour can be socially structured. Observing meetings of psychiatric staff, she was able to conclude that humour served to reinforce the social order.

22

In particular, humour flowed down the hierarchy of prestige and never up it: humour was directed (down) at subordinates and seldom (if ever) returned.

Humour was used as a strategy for coping with structural difficulties in this particular formal setting. At these meetings junior staff would report on therapeutic strategies they were using with mental patients. These junior staff were also graduate students and were being trained, so that their relations to the senior staff were multi-stranded. The senior staff were required to both correct and to encourage the junior staff. On the one hand, the senior staff were to provide guidance and instruction, which often meant criticism. On the other hand, they needed to provide support and assurance. One way around this structural dilemma was for the senior staff to deliver their criticisms cloaked in humour, which removed much of the sting of any censure. It is possible, too, that by involving all of those in the meeting in these comments through their collective laughter, that this might lead the junior staff to more assiduously carry out the advice they had been given since it had the weight of the collective spirit behind it.

This example shows how micro-level behaviour can clearly reflect the broader social structure of the hospital. This is particularly true in formal meeting situations. However, Mulkay (1988) argues that much humour in less structured situations is far less tied to social structure. Rose Coser's study is a classic, and other studies she has carried out also show clear effects of social structure in interaction situations – e.g. the different social structures of surgical and medical wards. Beyond these examples there are a myriad of studies which show how interaction patterns reflect the social structure of organisations.

Laughter may be rather more important than at first appears. People do indeed vary in their wittiness, but to a considerable extent laughter is shaped by the particularities of the social situation. This shapes who is supposed to crack the jokes, who is to be laughed at, and who one can laugh with. Social structure is clearly part of everyday life.

Social structure of a halls of residence

Social structure can also be found beyond the interactional level, in organisations and communities.

The earliest published sociological contribution of one of the most famous contemporary sociologists is a clear-cut evocation of a classical form of social structural analysis: Giddens's case-study of a university Halls of Residence (1960). In this study the formal structure of the Halls is laid out in terms of the relation between the Hall's authority-structure (centred on the Warden) and the several-layered student body, with its sharply differentiated year-by-year strata. The rituals which help sustain this official structure are discussed – especially the hissing used to sanction late-comers to the evening dinner. Later, comments are made on the way in which external social conditions limit or increase the Warden's power. Briefly, his power to expel badly behaved students is limited when it becomes more acceptable for students to live outside the halls (itself a condition facilitated by increasing numbers of students coming to the University). The Halls (at the stage of writing) had a relaxed attitude to students returning at night, but Giddens argues that rebuilding might result in the Halls being enclosed, which would then offer the Warden the opportunity to physically control the times at which gates would be locked and residents required to be home.

In a classic standard move common in structural analysis, Giddens complements the analysis of the formal social structure with a picture of the informal social structure: the 'underlife' through which the Hall's social life actually works. This involves delving into the network-structure within the Halls: especially those social patterns which arise from clique-formation. In turn, cliques are seen to be shaped by the caste-lines drawn by the formal social structure and also by the ecological living-arrangements of the various accommodation units within the halls. People who live together tend to form a clique (presumably) as a result of frequent mingling and the joint meeting of life's little challenges (e.g. providing 'suppers'). The potentially dire consequences of not being involved with a clique are underlined by Giddens: while some loners quite enjoy their social isolation, others may be ostracised, scapegoated and eventually expelled from the group.

As well as the basic social building-blocks of the cliques and the individual units of the Halls, Giddens also points to other dimensions of social structure, especially the differences accorded to those who have not come straight from secondary school, but have experienced either military service or work in the interim. Such background experience imported into the Hall's environment is not only recognised in student culture, but is clearly a social resource which can be drawn on in building power-bases. However, this dimension of the operation of the Halls is not well-developed in Giddens's analysis and he fails to follow up other possibly important social aspects (e.g. the fact that this is an all-male institution does not attract explicit attention!). However, in general, this is quite an exemplary example of structural analysis: expedited by the small-scale and semi-closed nature of the Halls. It is interesting, too, that formal methods of empirical study are not adopted (we are not even told such simple sociographic facts as the number of students in the Halls!), with Giddens relying solely on his own experiences.

This example shows the utility of social structural analyses in providing a framework for understanding one's own experiences, and avoiding assuming that social life is determined solely by the personalities of the people involved. With some experience of the social structure, and planned exploration of its further reaches, it is possible to construct an adequate model of the various social patternings involved. The resulting picture certainly renders a wider range of participant's behaviour understandable, but it retains a somewhat static, one-dimensional, 'box-like' feel to it.

Suicide in Samoa

In the 1980s there was a marked climb in suicide rates across many Pacific Island societies. It was difficult to be sure how much of this was real since the statistical apparatuses in such small-scale and recently-modernising societies were often incapable of producing high-quality data on such awkward social issues: especially where sensitivities (not the least religious ones concerning death) cloud the 'truth'. In a conference called to review this area of growing concern, both culturological and psychological explanations were parlayed by anthropologists on the one hand, and psychiatrists on the other. The former contemplated the cultural peculiarities of the different cultures involved and the extent to which they mandated or prohibited suicide as a 'legitimate' course of social action. At the other end of the scale, psychiatrists probed for individual differences and personality disorders which might result in heightened suicide.

Yet, the key to disentangling this social phenomenon seemed to lie very much 'in the middle' between culture and psychology, as it were, through a structural analysis of the Samoan situation at village level (Macpherson and Macpherson 1987). Many of the suicides could be fitted within an 'anomie' explanation, where suicide was seen as a socially-induced way of handling difficult social situations. The classic Mertonian anomie explanation suggests that deviant behaviour arises when a lower social class is trapped in a situation where its members' aspirations are frustrated through lack of legitimate access to the resources which would fulfil these aspirations. In the Samoan case, there was a generational twist, albeit one with some social class connotations. In many Samoan villages, a tradition-steeped gerontocracy of resource-controllers faces a younger generation with soaring aspirations for access to Western resources and often a lowered orientation and commitment towards traditional cultural patterns. Too often, members of the younger generation are required to labour in the gardens, without any attention to their needs for control over their own work practices, or the rewards of their labour in terms of access to resources. The younger generation feels the heels of the elderly pressed hard on their necks. Moreover, their options declined in the 1980s. Whereas earlier generations could at least temporarily migrate to surrounding white settler colonies and earn hard cash, severe migration restrictions now limit those possibilities.

This closing down of the range of choice, and the daily practices of subjugation, created bad feelings which easily erupted into nasty and public incidents. Sadly, many younger people who became embroiled in such incidents would commit suicide to recover their social honour *in absentia*. Clearly, this widespread form of suicide was very largely a totally unintended result of culturally-mandated social structural arrangements and their apparent inability to adapt in the face of changing social circumstances. There was a further implication which the Macphersons pursued. They argue that in those villages where there was a higher concentration of the elderly in relation to youth, there would be a higher likelihood of such structural clashes taking place. By calculating an age index for each village, they were able to show that structural variation among villages was indeed related to the likelihood of suicides: in 'aged' villages the suicide rate was much higher than among villages with 'younger' age-structures. While cultural and psychological differences clearly shape suicides, social structure can be shown to play a major role.

In this example, no attempt is made to map out the various dimensions of the social structure as a whole: it is only those aspects which are pertinent to providing an explanation of particular patterns of behaviour which are drawn on. But of course, they cannot be drawn on unless at least a more global understanding of the social structure as a whole is available to the analyst (as it clearly was in this particular example). The example shows most vividly that it can be relatively specific aspects of social structure which have major discernible effects; in this case, particular patterns of age-structure, reinforced by wider societal contexts. Moreover, this example shows that even in exotic societies, which we are often tempted to consider as integrated wholes, fine-tuned social structural analysis remains important.

Structures of scientific performance

The effects of social structures are not only seen within individual communities, but also in the pattern of relationships among whole sets of organisations.

Over a couple of centuries, the country whose scientists carried the 'standard' of highest scientific advance has changed from time to time. Whereas French scientists made the most productive work in the early nineteenth century, they were eclipsed by German scientists at the end of the nineteenth century, and by US scientists in this century. British science has had a more steady stream of scientific contribution, although largely fitting the French pattern. This changing pattern might be attributed to changes in the intelligence and creativity of scientists, or might reflect different emphases in the wider culture within which the scientists worked. However, in his widely-ranging study, Ben-David (1971 [1984]) was able to convincingly attribute differences in the scientific success of national arenas to the structural arrangements for scientific work.

The French scientific establishment has long been effective because it has pulled talent into a centralised matrix of scientific institutions based in Paris, and broadly controlled by part of the governmental machinery. However, this very centralisation often proved, in the long-run, to be cloying. The hierarchical organisation provided excellent apprenticeship situations, but precluded much initiative on the part of junior scientists.

Nor was there any alternative social structure arrangement within which precocious talent could be nurtured. Finally, the scientists in these institutions became inevitably, at least partially, cut-off from relevant developments in the wider world around them.

The German way of organising scientific work had several advantages. Whereas there remained an element of central control by a bureaucracy, each of a rather wider range of universities had some autonomy and there was some competition for prestige among them. In particular, the system allowed the gradual development of fresh departments in the interstitial areas where scientific advance seems most likely to occur. This was because the universities had the ability to institute new Chairs and for these to be assigned in areas not necessarily blessed with the aura of accepted respectability as a discipline. The regular arrangements requiring doctoral research study, and also discussion within 'seminars', broadened and toughened the rigours of argument. However, again, this structural arrangement proved stifling in the longer-run, since each little unit remained heavily authoritarian and hierarchical, with juniors forever shackled as assistants to the chair-holder.

By the mid-twentieth century, the USA dominated scientific achievement. Again, this lurch forward in productivity was accompanied by, and caused by, changed structural arrangements. In the USA, there are a huge number of universities, many of which compete with each other for prestige. In this task, they attempt to attract the most talented staff they can and are often innovative in providing the arrangements that 'star' faculty may wish for. The openness of the system is further facilitated by the relatively democratic way in which departments are organised (see Crothers 1991 for an alternative viewpoint). Chairs are dethroned to become essentially administrative positions, often held temporarily since carrying out administrative duties is not held in high regard. These structural arrangements better harness the energies of scientists of each age-grade and rank. And externally, the driving force of competition for prestige among scientists and between their host institutions is powerful. These contribute vitally to the success of US science, above and beyond its rich demographic and resource bases.

High suicide-rates are unfortunate not only for the individuals concerned, but also because they reflect badly on the social cohesion of the communities in which they occur: hopefully scientific advance has more beneficial effects on both individuals and their communities. Again, this example hammers home the point that it is not always just the amount of resources that are available, or the cultural values which pertain, that are central, but it may be the way in which these are organised into social structures. Different types of social structure can have quite different effects.

Demography

As study of social structures increases in scale, there are some difficulties that a single observer might experience in obtaining a wide enough angle of view. One way of handling this difficulty is to cut back on the details encompassed in the study.

One of the crudest and yet most powerful explanatory messages is delivered by the brute facts of demography, especially the ways in which people's life expectancies can be predicted from careful analysis of life-tables built up from collections of vital statistics. The average pattern of life-experiences can be relentlessly 'read off' such information, i.e. likelihood at particular ages (and often by sex or other factors) of:

- giving birth;
- marrying;
- producing children; and
- dying.

Such rates can vary sharply over time or occasionally swing crazily, but tend to have a concrete regularity over decades. People's life-chances in the aggregate can sometimes be calculated with a close accuracy.

While demography tends to only cover a limited range of phenomena, similar inexorable rates found in collectivities can be found over a much wider range of behaviour. For example, Durkheim (1952) was able to show that suicide rates in any one country remained quite constant over a long period, and also that they varied from country to country according to differences in social structure.

This example involves a very 'thin' view of social structure, involving only a few key social variables (age and gender) and a few basic processes, but it also points out the long-term effects of social structures quietly (as it were) working away behind the busy flux of everyday life. It also makes the point that an understanding of social structure is cumulative and obtaining a good description of the present demographic structure, and the growth implications inherent in it, is a vital early step in any structural analysis.

World-systems

Social science developed alongside the rise of industrial capitalism and also the vigorous elevation of the nation-state. It has often imported assumptions from these links. One of these assumptions has been the central social importance of the nation-state. In many studies, it is assumed that nations are discrete holistic units that can be readily compared with each other. However, the Annales school of French historians, and more particularly the world-systems viewpoint put forward by Wallerstein (e.g. Hopkins and

Wallerstein 1982) argue that over the last several centuries, if not millennium, many societies have been embedded within world-empires or world-systems, which have a very direct impact on their operation. Both of these sets of views are much inspired by Marx, while also operating within mainstream social science. The current world-system of capitalism stretches back to at least the sixteenth century. It differs from earlier world-empires in that it is not dominated by a single political unit, although one or other of several key states have been the most important from time to time.

The world-system has constantly been stratified into three layers: a core, a semi-periphery and a periphery (together with the outer ring of those areas of the world not yet incorporated into the world-system). However, the membership of particular countries or regions within each of these three categories has varied over time. Each layer plays a quite different economic role, and the whole system is organised so as to give advantage to those countries (or those parts of countries) which are in the core.

While nation-states are deeply etched in everyday experience and in much social science literature, it is also important to stand back and view the way they are shaped by wider systems. These wider systems, in turn, constitute a higher level of analysis in social structure.

The last of this handful of examples extends further the scale covered by the national-level demographic example, but adds in the grandeur of a long time-period and an account of socio-economic relations for good measure. Most sociologists work within a national frame of reference, sometimes without fully recognising this. Wallerstein's analyses show that there are clear, although not obvious, patterns working behind this level.

LESSONS

A few quick lessons might be won from the set of examples as a whole. Social structures are:

- highly varied;
- they operate at various levels from the world-system down to micro-level interactional contexts;
- cover a wide range of content; and
- depending on how they are put together, can be powerful or weak in their consequences (clearly, the examples chosen emphasise strong effects).

Often the effects of social structure work away, irrespective of cultural setting or individual differences of the people within them. Sometimes, quite stark contrasts between different structural arrangements can be seen, nicely illuminated by the analytical skills and presentational rhetoric of the analyst. However, many other structural effects remain shrouded within complexities and subtleties of social life, and we all cannot aspire to achieve the dramatic results of the more successful analyses.

29

But, of course, the power of social structural analysis does not rest with such a small group of examples, nor even the much larger pool of alternatives from which these few illustrations were taken. Our interest must lie in the more general and consolidated understandings of social structure which lie behind the several case studies which I have provided. After providing an historical account, the book moves on to examine the stock of more general understandings.

3

HISTORY OF SOCIAL STRUCTURAL ANALYSIS

PURPOSES OF THE CHAPTER

In this chapter, I review the history of the usages of the concept 'social structure'. To avoid trying to reproduce a full history of sociology and its related disciplines which this task must inevitably lead to, I focus quite narrowly on programmatic and general statements specifically concerning the term 'social structure'. Clearly, there is only space for highly limited accounts of the work of various theorists. My concern here is to try to capture the essence of their work and its precise salience for accounts of social structure, so that the huge outpourings of exegesis are treated but very lightly. After all, these discussions are merely pointers to areas for further reading.

A secondary purpose of the chapter is to lay out more information on which to build in further chapters. The historical material is also useful as a more readily digested introduction to some of the issues to be discussed later. The history is presented through treatment of successive 'cohorts' of social structural models. (For other, rather different historical accounts, see Alexander 1984; Leach 1968; Short 1986; Smelser 1988.)

As a preview, Table 3.1 provides a very broad map of the major approaches and their approximate time-periods. This framework is highly schematised and hardly reflects the much more considerable complexity actually involved.

Table 3.1 Phases in social structural thinking

Approach	Time-period
Founding fathers	1890–1920
British structural-functional anthropology	1920–1950
American structural-functional sociology	1950–1965
Inter-regnum	1965–1975
Structuralism	1975–1985
Process reconceptualisations	1985–present

THE CLASSIC TRADITION OF SOCIAL STRUCTURE ANALYSIS

The historical account provided in this chapter focuses on the more explicit formal presentations of concepts of social structure, which are particularly relevant to the development of theory concerning social structure. But alongside this more explicitly articulated stream of work, and beyond it too, there was a more informal development of ideas about social structure and employment of social structure analyses, if seldom labelled as such. Apart from this section, my account focuses on the visible layer of the iceberg. Here, attention is drawn to the less visible portion.

This might be considered a 'generic' social structure analysis, which can be particularly viewed through the eyes of C. W. Mills, who endeavoured to reconstruct some of its major principles (1960). Writers briefly mentioned earlier (through the definitions of social structure which they provided in Chapter 2), including De Tocqueville and Spencer, shared much of this view. This structural approach gradually evolved as a by-product of work in history, although it was also used in political analysis and more generally in social commentary. Interestingly, though, it was seldom connected with social research in the narrower sense.

Mills thought that sociology should connect the 'personal' with the collective, in his felicitous phrase that: 'The Sociological Imagination enables us to grasp history and biography and the relations between the two within society' (1959: 12). Even if Mills did not spell out an 'ideal typical' model of what a classical sociological analysis should involve, the conception can be 'read off' from his collection of exemplars (1960). Certainly, he indicated that classical analysis included 'basic conceptions or theories of such matters as social stratification and political authority, of the nature of bureaucracy and of capitalism, of the scale and drift of modern life, of the ambiguity of rationality, of the malaise individual men so often feel' (1960: 5). A classical sociological analysis focuses on at least one social grouping, but this is seen as being set within a wider social formation. These social groupings often have a particular economic role or position, hold power or are centrally involved with cultural development or maintenance. Examples would cover social classes, estates, broad political movements, or broad social positions concerned with culture (e.g. intelligentsia). The sociological analysis of such a social grouping examines:

- the trajectory of the grouping – its rise, maintenance and fall;
- the grouping's terminology (especially its own names for itself);
- internal positions and relations between them;
- external boundary maintenance;
- economic base;
- political power;
- cultural legitimacy;

- demography;
- social and ritual life;
- relations to other social groupings; and
- the leadership, organisations and networks through which it is organised, that can mobilise and achieve any common goals.

The more explicit models of social structure tend to build more formally on such informal models of social structure.

THE FOUNDING FATHERS

There clearly was a 'pre-history' of concepts of social structure. Several writers have drawn attention to the collectivist aspects of social theory in Greek, Roman, Arab, Medieval and Renaissance thought. On the other hand, there was a strong individualism built into the models of the classical political economists (such as the Scottish school, including Adam Smith) which clearly limited their interest in social structure. The individualism of this school has been grossly over-exaggerated in its later telling, which is unfortunate given its contemporary importance. However, it is inappropriate to pursue this historical topic here.

None of the now-recognised founding fathers of sociology had a well-developed explicit model of social structure, in any technical sense. However, a semi-implicit model of social structure was central within the work of each. For Marx and Weber in particular, this focused on class structure.

Marx

The main thrust of Marx's later work lay in understanding the economic machinery of capitalism. His 'sociology' is often not extracted from his broader 'political economy': moreover, it would be somewhat ironic to do so, since he would regard such separate treatment of components of social formations as limited. However, Marx's political economy was clearly placed within a broader social framework even if this social framework was more lightly sketched than the thoroughness accorded to the analysis of the central economic machinery.

Marx saw social life being lived within 'social formations'. These were composed of various economic, social and political groupings: especially social classes who were the main actors on the stage of history. In his views on classes, Marx was clearly aware of the distinction between 'class position' as such (as an 'empty box') and the persons occupying it at any particular time. As he says:

> To prevent possible misunderstanding, a word. I paint the capitalist and landlord in no sense *coleur de rose*. But here the individuals are dealt with

33

only in so far as they are the personifications of economic categories, embodiments of particular class-relations and class-interests.

(Marx 1971: xix)

Beyond this skeletal portrait of the basics of social structure, Marx elaborated a more complex social architecture, in which political entities and also ideological frameworks were built on the essential core of productive relations.

The specific economic form, in which unpaid surplus labour is pumped out of direct producers, determines the relationship of rulers and ruled, as it grows directly out of production itself and, in turn, reacts upon it as a determining element. Upon this, however, is founded the formation of the economic community which grows out of the production relations themselves, thereby determining simultaneously its specific political form. It is always the direct relationship of the owners of the conditions of production to the direct producers – a relationship always naturally corresponding with a definite stage in the development of the methods of labour and thereby its social productivity – which reveals the innermost secret, the hidden base of the entire social structure, and with it the political form of the relationship of sovereignty and dependence – in short, the corresponding specific form of the state.

(Marx 1971: vol. 3, 791)

In this way, Marx was able to build out from his view of the economy towards a more comprehensive understanding of the society. As well as indicating how the role of the state fitted into the basically capitalistic nature of modern social formations, ideology was given a key role. The ideas of the dominant class were seen as cloaking capitalist society in a blanket of 'false consciousness' which hid the way in which society was organised in their interests.

In addition to this relatively static picture of the structured relations between economy, polity and ideological aspects, Marx made various comments on the dynamics of the whole formation. An important point was the extent to which social groupings might cohere sufficiently to exert social power in their own right. A key difference is the one between a 'class-in-itself' (not aware of the shared nature of its material interests) and a 'class-for-itself' (which is aware of its shared interests and has some organisational capacity for realising these). A critical element in building the conflict necessary for an eventual revolution is the dissipation of the 'false consciousness' and its replacement with a 'revolutionary consciousness'.

In turn, the micro-dynamics of structural change are placed within a much wider historical framework in which the successive development of different modes of production are placed within a sequence. In a general way, ancient (slave), medieval (feudal) and modern (capitalist) modes are seen as part of an evolutionary sequence, which may then lead on to the subsequent stage of a socialist mode of production. Debate has raged over the extent to which this sequence is seen as a necessary one driven by an iron-clad law of historical determinism, rather than a more general historical framework in which the only relationship between modes is that subsequent modes are nurtured within previous ones, and in which later modes are built on the detritus of the resources and culture deposited by earlier modes. Marx's emphasis on the conditional nature of social science, such as his insistence on the limitation of the scope of much of his analysis to capitalist societies, strongly suggests that the sequence should be seen as contingent rather than deterministic.

For any mode of production, a long-term development sequence is suggested. Societal change is seen as driven from the interaction between economic organisational arrangements (relations of production) and technology (productive forces).

> At a certain stage of development, the material productive forces of society come into conflict with the existing relations of production ... from forms of development of the productive forces these relations turn into their fetters. Then begins an epoch of social revolution. The changes in the economic foundation lead sooner or later to the transformation of the whole immense superstructure.
>
> (Marx 1959: 21)

From a viewpoint even more broad than his socio-economic framework, much of Marx's earlier work includes comments about the social nature of mankind. Such broad comments about the essential nature of mankind are often referred to as contributions to 'philosophical anthropology'. Marx's comments have a dual focus: how people are linked together and the relation of individuals to their collective social arrangements. The first of these points is captured in the notion that mankind's most important relationship is with nature and in the creative production of commodities from it: *homo faber*. By nature mankind is in interaction with the material world, in order to eat. It is in the nature of mankind to produce things.

This, in turn, leads to an important point about the relation of individuals to the products they have produced. Marx argues that if individuals are not fully involved in the details of the production of commodities and both own and control the production process, this will result in 'alienation': feelings of separateness and apartness from their own products, often leading as a result to feelings of alienation from other people.

Needless to say, Marx's sociology has been endlessly interpreted, extended, revised and debated, and it is impossible to try to trace the multifarious threads up until the present. In broad terms, Marx's conception of society is generally compatible with almost all of most contemporary social structural analysis. However, for the most part, a classical Marxist position has little interest in the details of the operation of the 'surface' social structure. Instead, emphasis is placed on central political economic mechanisms which operate below the level of social structure as it is usually conceived. Such central

35

mechanisms focus on the exploitation built into economic arrangements. The social structure is essentially the container within which (perhaps more evocatively 'underneath' which) social change is effected. Sociologists tend to concentrate on other mechanisms and see the social order as less of an epiphenomenon, and therefore as more significant in itself. Yet, the broad framework in which Marx worked, including his philosophical anthropology, his political economy and his long-term historical concerns, are also particularly relevant for later sociologists.

Weber

Weber's views on social structure are more developed, and his theoretical reflections directly pertain to social structure. Nevertheless, Weber does not attempt to develop a full understanding of social structures. Rather, his structural analysis tools are designed to assist in the analysis of those portions of historical experience that he has a particular interest in. On the other hand, his work is cast within a very broad comparative and historical range: encompassing as it does aspects of the development of Western, Chinese, Indian and Ancient civilisations.

A central point in Weber's approach to social structure is his 'methodological individualism': he requires explanations to be spelled out in terms of the involvement of individuals. Rather than reifying social structures, he focuses attention on meanings, individual motivation and behaviour. He also takes a balanced position and requires sociological explanations to meet the criteria of providing 'objective' as well as 'meaningful' explanation. This creates a considerable tension in his sociological work between the broad sweep of his historical and comparative sociology, and his methodological writings which focus more on ideal types of behaviour at an individual level.

In one passage in his writings, Weber sketches how a sociological explanation might be built. The goal of a sociological analysis is to explain how given types of society came into being and continue to exist. This is to be pursued in two stages. As a preliminary investigation, a description of particular roles (Weber uses the term in passing but more generally refers to typical actors or individuals) must be developed:

> It is necessary to know what a 'king', an 'official', an 'entrepreneur', a 'procurer', or a 'magician' does; that is, what kind of typical action, which justifies classifying an individual in one of these categories, is important and relevant for an analysis, before it is possible to undertake the analysis itself.
>
> (Weber 1947: 107)

The sociological analysis proper then explains why individuals in these categories carry out typical actions in terms of patterns of individual motives.

As well as providing this broad analytical machinery, Weber developed rather more definitive concepts in the area of class structure. Weber's approach to social classes is much more multi-dimensional and flexible than Marx's, and a class is seen as any social grouping which shares a similar position within a market (e.g. the labour market), with 'similar position' meaning that its members share similar life-chances. Rather than emphasising only the economic/material sphere, Weber sees *several* dimensions around which social strata might form:

- class (concerned with economic matters);
- party (concerned with power);
- status-group (concerned with social prestige or honour).

Finally, for present purposes, Weber provided a particularly potent model of organisational analysis (and social structure more generally) with his model of a 'bureaucracy'. This he depicted as a 'machine' of hierarchically-organised 'offices' filled by meritocratically-appointed, salaried, careerist 'officials' who are constrained to efficiently tackle their collective tasks, within a systematic framework of rules, records and reporting. A bureaucracy is under the general responsibility of 'masters' outside its ranks (e.g. politicians, boards of directors). While this view clings too closely to the 'official theory' of many formal organisations, it nevertheless provides an interesting example of what a sociological model of a social grouping might contain.

While this more flexible approach provides an analytical purchase across a wide range of circumstances, it has some difficulties because of the very looseness of its stipulations. This has led to much terminological disputation, but has guided rather less empirical work.

Durkheim

Of the three founding fathers, Durkheim was the one most seriously concerned with social structure. However, even for Durkheim the precise term is used only in passing, and references are usually made more generally to society and the social bonds constituting society.

Durkheim provided an aggressive statement of an anti-reductionist, collectivist approach in sociology. The concept of a 'social fact' was central in his approach, and social facts were seen as separate from (and overwhelming) the individual.

'Social facts' are a framework of collectively shared obligations on the individual, either 'crystallised' (e.g. expressed in adages or writing) or more diffuse 'social currents'. Usually the collective shaping of a person is internalised and constant social pressure is not needed. Such social pressure is felt most when the obligations are resisted by a person, which results in conformity to them then being upheld by social groups or the state. Under this pressure, individuals have little choice but to buckle under.

At a more descriptive level, Durkheim developed a conception of 'social

37

morphology' involving accounts of the nature (e.g. size, functions), number, arrangement (e.g. spatial distribution) and interrelations (e.g. modes of communication, movement and mutual obligation) among the social parts (individual or collective) of a society. But as Turner and Beeghley (1981: 337; see also Andrews 1993) point out, Durkheim then did not in fact employ this schema in any actual analyses. Nevertheless, this is a conception stressing a quite concrete and spatially-grounded dimension of society which is later drawn on by some analysts (particularly the human ecologists).

Durkheim is particularly important for having clearly postulated (what I see as) the conceptual problem central to analysing social structures: what its 'division of labour' is, and what consequences this has for the structure's type and level of social integration. This issue is central to two of his major contributions. Whereas primitive social structures were seen as being organised in terms of everyone having similar tasks (which was complemented by tight 'repressive' social control), more complex societies have a division of labour characterised by complementary specialisation, and this is then matched by a system of social control which emphasises 'restitution'.

Durkheim's study of suicide (1952) was similarly concerned with the ways social structures generated this apparently highly individualistic act. Durkheim observed the relative steadiness of suicide rates in any region or country and postulated that the differential level of suicide between regions or countries was explained by the degree of social integration in each. Tight social organisation tends to suppress the suicide rate.

Yet, there is an odd lack of social structure in Durkheim's views, in that he posited little between the overarching 'moral order' of the whole society and the individual. Durkheim did point to the ritual significance of some performances and to the integrative importance of occupational groups. Otherwise, his social landscape was rather underpopulated.

Simmel

Of other sociologists in the 'founding' generation, the work of Simmel, in particular, has proved to be of lasting significance. At a more micro level, Simmel developed a 'formal' sociology (as opposed to sociological treatment of 'content') in which properties of small groups and social situations were seen to affect behaviour. This approach provided for the development of a sociology which would compile systematic propositions about the operation of social structures. For example, Simmel wrote about the effects of differences in sizes of groups for interaction among their members. The conception of abstracting social content across diverse situations in order to reveal structural similarities also proved to be helpful to later analysts.

Simmel's concept of 'forms' is an early statement of this view:

Social groups which are the most diverse imaginable in purpose and general significance may nevertheless show identical forms of behaviour toward one another on the part of individual members. We find superiority and subordination, competition, division of labour, formation of parties, representation, inner solidarity coupled with exclusiveness toward the outside, and innumerable similar features in the state, in a religious community, in a band of conspirators, kin, an economic association, in an art school, in the family. However diverse the interests are that gave rise to these sociations, the forms in which the interests are realised may yet be identical.

(Simmel, cited in Turner and Beeghley 1981: 273)

Simmel's imagery of the way in which people in modern societies are complexly related through cross-cutting social circles, as opposed to the concentric circles of more primordial situations, has proved fruitful for later thinking (e.g. it is a central metaphor used in Blau's work).

By the end of this period of rapid development of sociological ideas, many of the basic building blocks for later work had been laid down. Yet, strangely, at this stage there was no explicit, let alone shared, views on what the concept might comprise.

BRITISH STRUCTURAL-FUNCTIONAL ANTHROPOLOGY

Beginning in the late 1920s, and maturing in the immediate post-World War II period, a particular and self-conscious analytical approach to social structural analysis was developed by the British school of structural-functionalists. This approach was started by Malinowski, but predominantly shaped by Radcliffe-Brown, and was later summarised in a wider range of texts by leading British commentators, and in Nadel's theoretical treatise (1957). This fairly tightly organised school rejected earlier approaches in which emphasis was placed on the evolution and diffusion of cultural traits. Instead, their emphasis lay in understanding the current operation of small-scale societies (and later, rather larger African ones). Therefore, any social practice was seen in terms of its role within its societal context. 'Strange' tribal practices could be 'mapped' onto more commonly-understood Western concepts. This approach was considerably inspired by Durkheim's views on social collectivities, so that social practices were seen as enhancing or inhibiting the global integration of a society.

The approach has several assumptions or key distinctions:

- the importance of close understanding through 'participant observation';
- a separation of the time-bound flux associated with the surface form ('social organisation') compared to the relatively unchanging underlying forms ('structural forms');
- the difference, yet interpenetration, between culture and society;

39

- the importance of examining the interrelationships between social institutions and their importance ('functions') for the social whole;
- seeing kinship (and political/administrative structures) as the central institutions of societies (see Firth 1964).

Unfortunately, at the heart of its explanatory approach sits the functionalist fallacy: it is incorrect to explain something in terms of its consequences, unless a feedback mechanism linking consequences with causes can be found. However, this framework is a useful heuristic to guide hypotheses.

To develop appropriate explanations, the merely ornamental (which was often 'cultural') or the superficial peculiarities of any particular configuration (the 'social organisation') had to be set aside from the properly (socially) structural. Gellner captures the key distinction between culture and society and the associated denigration of studies of culture: 'structure was, for instance, whom one could marry; culture was what the bride wore' (1985: 136).

A classic example (see Cohen 1968: 42) of Radcliffe-Brown's approach concerns the 'joking' relationship between uncle (mothers' brother) and nephew (sisters' son) in South African patrilineal societies. There is a clash between the principles of seniority (being of an older generation) and of lineage (where relationships with members of the mothers' lineage are affectionate and permissive). This tension between the two clashing principles is managed by this 'joking relationship' (this closely compares with Coser's analysis of the social function of laughter sketched out in Chapter 2).

Although this British approach contrasted with more eclectic US approaches in cultural anthropology, over time it came to not only dominate British social anthropology, but also was generally suffused throughout US anthropology as well. As Murphy remarked in the early 1970s: 'Indeed, the proponents of the sociological view have won the day so thoroughly in both Britain and the United States that one could well present a strong case for the need to engage once again in cultural historical studies' (1972: 17).

The school had at least two main strands, with Malinowski endeavouring to reach down to the ways societies met the socio-biological needs of their members, while Radcliffe-Brown (1948) emphasised a more strictly social structural level of analysis. Indeed, there was some mutual distancing of the two principal proponents from each other's position.

Since the heyday of this approach, British social anthropology has been supplemented by a myriad of subsequent influences (e.g. Marxism, cultural structuralism, network studies, and frameworks which brought into question the relation between tribal societies and colonial powers). Nevertheless, many anthropological field studies, and the explanations erected on their results, still retain much of the central thrust of the structural-functional approach. It fits too neatly with the societal situation of small-scale tribal societies to be readily dispensed with.

AMERICAN STRUCTURAL-FUNCTIONAL SOCIOLOGY

The two strands

During the 1950s and 1960s, US sociology was dominated by an approach generally labelled as 'structural-functionalist' or (retrospectively in Mullins 1973) as 'Standard American Sociology' (SAS). To a considerable extent, this involved a translation and adaptation of British structural-functional anthropology into a contemporary and larger-scale US context. The anthropological approach was also generalised to social systems at all scales, including small groups.

The common labelling of this approach tends to over-emphasise the role of the functional mode of explanation (whereby a social phenomenon is understood in relation to its consequences, especially consequences for higher-order social systems of which the component is a part). As with its anthropological predecessor, this particular explanatory tactic is not crucial, and functions rather as a heuristic approach for generating hypotheses.

Under the shelter of this conceptual umbrella, there was a strong and consistent attention to the analysis of social structure. This was accomplished in two main ways. One was through the development of research tools for investigating social structures. Another path lay in the development of concepts such as 'role theory' and 'social system', and a range of other concepts relating to social structure which were widely deployed. Theoretical and methodological advances often benefited each other. I will illustrate briefly each of these two paths in turn.

Standard American Sociology (SAS)

A strong propulsion to employing concepts of social structure in sociological studies came through an alliance with burgeoning survey research, in which a range of standard social background variables were routinely deployed in surveys to see which were useful in predicting patterns of behaviour or attitudes. Such sets of social background variables, once aggregated, form a useful operationalisation of social structure. As Merton pointed out long ago, these social background variables reflected the main social statuses which people might occupy:

> The categories of audience measurement have . . . been primarily those of income stratification (a kind of datum obviously important to those ultimately concerned with selling and marketing their commodities), sex, age and education (obviously important for those seeking to learn the advertising outlets most appropriate for reaching special groups). But since such categories as sex, age, education and income happen also to correspond to some of the chief statuses in the social structure, the

41

procedures evolved for audience measurement by the students of mass communication are of direct interest to the sociologist as well.

(Merton 1968 [1949]: 505)

This operationalisation of the components and effects of social structure involved describing a range of people's attitudes and behaviour in terms of which social background variables they were most associated with. For example, is voting for one political party, rather than another, structured by social class, ethnicity, gender or attitudes? This produces a sophisticated description of how different parts of the overall society are linked to the infinite profusion of behaviours and attitudes. Such a quantitative and empirically-based approach is necessary given the far-flung and large-scale nature of modern societies, where observers can only occupy the smallest of niches in particular pockets of the whole social enterprise. In these larger arenas, resorting to survey methods seems imperative.

While much of this sociology retained a strong interest in characteristics of individuals (or patterns among various of the properties of individuals) which the survey research methodology made possible, surveys were also employed to study characteristics of various types of social unit. Thus, social entities such as groups, households/families, organisations, suburbs, regions and nations were also regularly studied in a fashion analogous to the respondents in a survey: data was systematically collected for each unit and then the pooled data searched for interesting patterns which might reveal the workings of social structure.

As well, considerable theoretical and methodological knowledge accumulated about how relations between individuals and various types of social entities might best be studied and explained. For example, the concept of the 'ecological (or aggregative) fallacy' was developed. Further methodological work indicated the conditions under which it was reasonable or unreasonable to infer from one level of social structure to another.

There were also a variety of more specific approaches such as:

- 'human ecology' as formalised by Duncan and Schnore (1959) in their 'POET' framework which involved four areas for description and analysis, together with their interrelations: Population, Organisation, Environment and Technology;
- The 'Resource Mobilisation Theory' (RMT) approach to the study of social movements which reflected on the experiences of the new social movements (black, women's, environmental, peace, sexual preference, handicapped etc.) and explained patterns associated with successful as opposed to unsuccessful protest-group social movements (see section on resource mobilisation in Chapter 5, pp. 117–19);
- Kuhn's studies of social identities (e.g. 1960) through the 'Who am I? Twenty statement test' which explored the ways in which people organised their various sub-identities;

42

- at a more macro-sociological level, those 'social cleavages' identified that were more salient in describing patterns of societal development and operation, e.g. voting patterns; and
- role theory, which was considerably developed (as described in Chapter 5).

This diverse assemblage constituting SAS formed very successful operational conceptual and research tools for exploring large-scale, multi-faceted social structures – in particular, social features within the USA. A version of social structural analysis had been routinised and could be readily deployed in any situation. During the 1950s and 1960s, this approach guided a thorough descriptive working over of the social organisation of almost all areas of US social life. It was then emulated, as the concepts and methodologies of SAS spread, by European and then developing-country sociologists.

Much of the development of theoretical work in SAS was closely driven by empirical studies, and sometimes by policy issues. Explicit development of theory was held to be important, although only a piecemeal patch of partial formulations was ever available. Usually, the theory for any particular study was fashioned, from the general theoretical resources available, to suit the findings that had been already obtained, although occasionally studies would be carried out to test theoretical notions directly. An example of the former style of developing theory was the way Hyman, Merton and others dug out the concept of 'reference group' from review of, and reflection upon, a large heap of studies from US Army social research in World War II (see Merton 1949 [1968]).

However, in the longer-term this more empirically-orientated SAS approach has tended to run out of steam, and both have faded in popularity. Part of the difficulty lay in the limitations of the conceptualisations of social structure that were being used, and part of the difficulty lay in the open-ended nature of this enterprise. The possible patterns of behaviour and attitudes that could be researched is infinite. There are thousands of attitudinal and behavioural variables and a wide range of social background variables to relate to these, not to mention the myriad causal paths that might be traced within this enormous array. There seemed no easy way of achieving any closure. Explanations tended to get *ad hoc* and lengthy. The conceptual armament available to analysts provided general guidance, but few specific, explicit predictions. Any cumulation of experience and theoretically-significant findings seemed limited and hard-won. There was a 'retreat into the present' in which longer-term and wider-scale social contexts tended to be ignored. Studies conducted in the limited context of contemporary USA were presented as being 'universally' applicable, although this tendency was somewhat counteracted by the international comparative social science research movement which did harness similarly-obtained findings from other countries.

Talcott Parsons

Alongside the wide-ranging 'middle order theorising' which accompanied the SAS studies, the 'grand theoretical' work of Talcott Parsons dominated the theoretical stage. This schema has been the subject of hundreds of commentaries, so at present I need only sketch its major features which include:

- the development of what is termed a general theory of 'action', i.e. meaningful behaviour by individuals;
- distinctions between three key, inter-linked master-concepts: those of culture, social systems and personality (see especially Kroeber and Parsons 1958; Ogles and Parsons 1959; Parsons 1973);
- social systems which are seen as the interaction of the plurality of persons and their relationships, with its central building-block being that of the role;
- a four-level hierarchical classification of types of social unit: particular roles, collectivities (clusters of roles), norms (of social categories, e.g. those relevant to gender) and values (of the society in general);
- a strong tendency to see higher levels (e.g. values) as 'steering' the lower levels;
- a depiction of cultural values as falling along positions on each of four main polarities: diffuseness vs. specificity, particularism vs. universalism, affectivity vs. affective neutrality, quality vs. performance; and
- these same emphases (now called 'pattern variables') are also held to shape how interactions with others are handled.

Within this broader framework, a systems analysis was later added, which involved an analytical division of the social system, according to the 'AGIL scheme', into four further sub-systems involving:

- adaptation (the problem of securing sufficient resources for goal achievement, e.g. the 'economy');
- goal-attainment (setting and achieving long-term goals, e.g. the 'polity');
- integration (the problem of securing the mutual adjustment of the elements of the system, achieved through the 'societal community', e.g. legal institutions, system of social stratification, medical care); and
- latency (the problem of pattern-maintenance and tension management in the face of changes – the 'fiduciary', e.g. cultural institutions, religion, socialising agencies).

In a further analytical step each sub-system was seen as the home-base for a particular 'generalised media of exchange' which circulated around the whole social system, comprising:

- money (based in the economy);
- power (based in the polity);

- labour commitments (based in the fiduciary); and
- influence (based in the societal community).

Finally, Parsons has a view about the long-term process of change which he sees as a progress towards the ever-finer specialisation of institutions, together with the development of integrative institutions to cope with the resultant increasing needs of system integration.

In this later approach, societies are seen as sub-systems producing and exchanging these various media, although Parsons nevertheless still retains his strong emphasis on the importance of cultural values.

In terms of this system, a sociological understanding of any particular institution (e.g. a school or church) can be gained by 'locating' them as falling into one (or other) of these sub-systems. (Institutions, in turn, were subdividable into the same set of sub-systems.) Of course, things are seldom so simple, so that many social institutions can be multi-functional and any given sub-system may span several institutions: this is not handled very clearly in Parsons' approach. Another over-simplified aspect is Parsons' too-ready assumption that more detailed levels of interaction were fairly simply shaped by higher-order social systems.

Parsons' approach has been subject to much criticism and commentary. Readers find much difficulty with the overly formalistic theory style with its complex structures of multiple boxes, and also with the strange emptiness of people among its cells. A frequent refrain is that 'there is no action in the theory of action'. And certainly, despite its comprehensive range, it fails to cover everything.

Although many of Parsons' points are redolent for later theoretical work, his framework has now largely fallen out of favour. (Several contemporary theorists, including Habermas, Luhmann and Alexander, have been influenced by Parsons, but have moved his theory on in different directions.)

It was a pity that Parsons' theoretical system and SAS did not fit better together and establish tighter links. Oddly, they have opposite faults, and so a compromise might have suited them both. Since SAS was insufficiently theoretical and too open-ended, it could have been nicely balanced by the Parsonian theoretical system which was remarkably 'data-free' and too rigidly closed. Despite these various faults, there are still many lessons to be won from the social structural analyses of this 'golden era' of sociological thinking.

AN INTER-REGNUM?

By the late 1960s and early 1970s, the conceptualisations used in SAS not only began to wane in popularity, but were also directly attacked. Micro-sociologists were concerned that SAS required too formal and reified a view of people's relationships to the social structure: an 'over-socialised' conception of mankind (to use the title of Dennis Wrong's famous article in 1961). On the other hand, the SAS structural analysts were criticised for dealing too often with trivia, for ignoring major societal-level phenomena outside the framework they were working within, for lack of any historical or comparative perspective, and for an implicit conservative support of the *status quo*.

SAS was judged by many to be at least partially successful in providing an interesting sociology, but by now some of its achievements were beginning to look a bit threadbare, and more alluring alternative approaches began to crowd around to attract sociological attention.

The critique of SAS as being overly concerned with 'consensus' was consolidated for a decade or so through the development of a supposedly polar-opposite 'conflict' view: a 'soft-core' Marxism. This contrast was useful for mobilising alternative emphases, but a sharp distinction between consensus and conflict models proved difficult to sustain over the longer term as it came to be realised that the two approaches could be seen as essentially complementary, and indeed sharing an underlying view of social structure.

One book published in this period had an immediate (but not long-lasting) effect. This was because it summarised much of the symbolic interactionist micro-level critique of SAS, and yet did not dilute the power of this critique by only looking at micro-situations. Berger and Luckmann (1966) developed a sophisticated account of the 'social construction of reality' which outflanked and advanced the treatments then available. The revolutionary impact of their work seems to have long since faded, although their schema still holds contemporary interest. Their general position emphasised the fragility of social reality and the involvement of people in constructing the social structures they then came to experience as solid and real. A major thrust in their analysis is the way social structures are organised to cover any broaches to their facticity. Lines of defence include the sharing of experiential commonalities, the deployment of aphorisms and sayings, and then relating difficulties to broader underlying conceptualisations. This approach points to the major role of large-scale, legitimating cultural structures, such as religion, which serve to secure the social structure. Interestingly, theirs is not a social psychology as many analysts taking a 'social constructivism' view might have moved to. Rather, Berger and Luckmann take a macro-sociological approach.

The SAS approach has continued within sociology (especially in North American sociology) and many social science journals remain filled with studies carried out within its broad paradigm. It has not only survived, but has continued to develop. Many of these developments endeavour to redress some of the difficulties of the earlier (classical SAS) approach. Common rhetoric in these more sophisticated versions of SAS cleaves to the formal, mathematical and statistical aspects of social structure. As a result, their work can become inaccessible; thus they have become rather detached from the mainstream of sociological attention. (Some of these studies are picked up again in the later section reviewing contemporary work on social structure.)

Another link forward from this earlier period has occurred over the last decade, under the leadership of Alexander (and in the writing of several important Continental social theorists, including Habermas and Luhman) – namely, a 'neo-functionalist' revival (e.g. Alexander 1985) which has attempted to reclaim much of theoretical territory earlier dominated by Parsons.

STRUCTURALISM

During the late 1960s, there were two forms of structural analysis which captured much attention, both drawing inspiration from Marxism and both emanating from Paris (Glucksmann 1974). Despite their relatively brief span of popularity, both marked out the extremes of a 'structural determinist' approach, and so have been pivotal in the subsequent development of thinking about social structure. Much recent thinking about social structure has been a reaction – often an extreme reaction – against this high tide of structuralism.

Lévi-Strauss

For French anthropological theorist Claude Lévi-Strauss, 'The term "social structure" has nothing to do with empirical reality but with models built up after it' (1963: 279). Indeed, the drive of his analysis is to show how the styles of 'native' thinking (in whichever culture is being studied) across all areas of cultural and social life are embedded within deep semi-linguistic patterns of thinking (possibly even mentalistic: being hard-wired into the digital structure of the brain). Thus, native concepts of kinship patterns, religious ideology and all else are subsumed under broad models of thinking that eventually reduce down, via transformation rules, into dualities in people's heads.

> Primitives and moderns, alike, attempt to develop coherent schemes, or conscious models of society, that give meaning and order to their activities, but their thoughts strain in the direction of distortion and mystification because of self-involvement and the limitations of human conceptual ability.... Underlying the conscious models, however, are mental infrastructures or unconscious models, which are the mainsprings of human thought and which are isomorphic with the structures of underlying social phenomena. These unconscious models are frequently obscured...by the conscious models which may appear...to give sufficient explanation of the phenomena being studied.
>
> (Murphy 1972: 110)

47

Even if this approach no longer drives many social structural analyses, it has raised important questions about the way the structure of the mind might in turn shape our social and cultural apparatus.

Althusser

The other structuralist development, which peaked at much the same time, was centred on the work of social philosopher Louis Althusser. In this approach of 'structural Marxism', Marx was (re)interpreted to fit a highly determinist and scientific understanding of social development. Very strong emphasis was placed on the concept that the development of a scientific Marxism required a sharp separation from prior, pseudo-scientific approaches which remained blinded by ideological bias. Even the more humanistic 'philosophical anthropology' of Marx's earlier writings were to be sequestered as 'pre-scientific'.

Marx's model of the working of the capitalist economy was accepted as adequate (indeed, Althusser was not very concerned to peer into the details of the economic machinery postulated by Marx). Instead, attention focused on two consequent issues:

1 how Marxism might be construed to offer satisfactory explanations of types of society other than capitalist (and indeed to provide a theorised sequence of types of society); and
2 how the whole of a society was to be seen as operating (given that, as I noted above, Marx's views on this are but sketchily developed).

The answers given on these two issues are interrelated. A three-fold distinction of any society is promulgated: the economy, the polity and the ideological apparatus. The functional role of the latter two sectors is to repress the population by force and through consensus into supporting the *status quo* of the current mode of economic organisation.

This distinction is then used in two ways. Any society can be described in terms of which of the three structures is dominant. However, no matter which is the dominant structure, it is always the economic structure that determines which is dominant: the economy is the determinant 'in the last instance'. In capitalism, the economy is the main institution, whereas earlier societies had been dominated by the family or by feudal political and religious institutions. Others in this school further developed heavily theoretical models of society.

There has been a definite, if diffuse, continuing influence in sociology of the Althusserian, and to a lesser extent the Lévi-Straussian, programmes. Undoubtedly they helped to raise the quality of theoretical work in social structural analysis. However, some social theorists have regarded these French developments as quite strange, and moved to quickly distance themselves from them: e.g. Blau's work on attempting to consolidate approaches is replete with

48

ritual aloofness from Lévi-Strauss's denial that sociological models are other than in the observer's mind.

Blau's attempted synopsis and programme

In 1975, Blau organised a group of eminent US social theorists to directly confront the concept of 'social structure'. These included several sociologists involved in historically orientated or comparative studies, rather than the more common use of social structure in survey and other empirical work (as in the SAS programme described above). These chapters are useful statements of various approaches to social structure.

In addition, Blau's own summary chapter, which actively seeks to classify the key aspects of the other chapters, provides a useful overview of some of the different dimensions which characterised the concepts of social structure which were held at that time. His definition is that: 'Social structure refers to the patterns discernible in social life, the regularities observed, the configurations detected' (1975: 3).

Blau sees the various models of social structure, in each of the twelve chapters provided by the invited contributors, as involving different combinations of choice along six planes, which he groups into four dimensions. These include:

- the level at which the picture of social structure is pitched (micro vs. meso vs. macro);
- the time dimension involved (evolutionary vs. historical vs. ahistorical);
- abstractness of theoretical approach (universalistic vs. particularistic);
- the view of what is the antithesis of structure (chaos vs. randomness vs. absence of external constraints);
- mental images of the patterning of structure (configuration of positions vs. set of substrata or axes of differentiation vs. configurations of relations);
- the driving causal forces (psychological vs. internal to social structure vs. external conditions).

This schema seems a useful way of comparing alternative approaches to social structure (although the original schema needs to be developed to be more useful). What is even more interesting, though, is that when Blau classified each of the twelve authors in the symposium in terms of these dimensions, he found very little similarity, let alone much consensus. Rather, each theorist made different choices on each of the dimensions. This suggests that there is a considerable range of viewpoints on social structure, even during an era when sociology was seen as being particularly coherent.

A few years later, in 1978, Blau was again responsible for organising sessions on 'Varieties of Structural Inquiry', this time at the World Congress of Sociology in Uppsala, Sweden. (These were published in 1981 and co-edited with Robert K. Merton.) This collection is much more diverse than the earlier one, and the attempt to forge a synthetic framework for them is correspond-ingly less well developed. Blau notes (1981: 9) the differences between the contributors to this second volume in terms of their position on:

• relationship between culture and social structure;
• ontology of social structure (whether it exists in reality or only as a model);
• relationship between positions and social relations;
• emphasis on form vs. content;
• defining attributes (e.g. consensus vs. conflict).

However, this time he does not endeavour to classify the various contributors in terms of his schema.

Instead, Blau discerns a common denominator: '...that social structure refers to those properties of an aggregate that are emergent and that conse-quently do not characterise the separate elements composing the aggregate' (Blau and Merton 1981: 9). Examples of emergent structural properties are:

• sociometric networks and group cohesion;
• the shape of the hierarchy of authority, the degree of centralisation of decision-making and division-of-labour within an organisation (as opposed to its component work-groups etc.);
• the form of government and the economic institutions of a nation (as opposed to its component communities, organisations and regions).

His example of what does not constitute an emergent structural property is 'average IQ or median education' since these are properties of an aggregate of individuals. However, while Blau is undoubtedly right to point to the low-level of collectivisation involved with such individualised characteristics, these can nonetheless be pertinent aspects of a social grouping.

As well as these attempts at integration of the work of other structural theorists, Blau has pursued his own programme of structural analysis, which he has termed a 'primitive theory of social structure' (and which is discussed in Chapter 5). This is part of a theoretical movement which is pursuing a programme of 'radical structuralism'. Of other proponents of this view, Mayhew (1981) is clearly the most extreme. They take the view that it is unnecessary to understand social meaningfulness, and that social structural analysis should be pursued by grimly sticking to sheer objective structural features, in what is held out to be a strongly collectivist, structuralist view.

PROCESS RE-CONCEPTUALISATIONS OF SOCIAL STRUCTURE

Imageries of social structure

By the late 1970s, the critique of ideas about social structure had turned in a much more strictly theoretical direction. The advantages of this trend were that it began to lay the foundation for more sophisticated understandings of social structure. Unfortunately, the consequences of this trend seemed to assist in the very demise of interest in 'social structure'! The topic became detached from concern with social issues and social theorists were uninterested in linking their work with analyses of existing social structures. Instead, the theoretical work was driven either by exegesis of classical texts or by the wash of philosophical issues imported from outside sociology.

Several recent theorists have touched on the concept of social structure. However, many have confined themselves to projecting an imagery of social structure which is not developed at length: such as the word-picture provided by Norbert Elias (see also Mouzelis 1993):

> The network of interdependencies among human beings is what binds them together. Such interdependencies are the nexus of what is here called figuration, a structure of mutually oriented and dependent people. Since people are more or less dependent on each other first by nature and then through social learning, through education, socialisation and socially generated reciprocal needs, they exist . . . only as pluralities, only in figurations. That is why . . . it is not particularly fruitful to conceive of men in the image of individual man. It is more appropriate to envisage an image of numerous interdependent people forming figurations.
>
> (Elias 1978: 261)

Two major theorists have brought out in-depth discussions of social structure: Bourdieu's 'social constructivism' and Giddens' 'structuration theory'. Each deserves a brief summary.

Bourdieu

Bourdieu has developed a sophisticated and appealing imagery of social structure and has connected this up with a wide range of empirical studies of particular social structures. (See especially Bourdieu 1992; Calhoun *et al*. 1993.) As with other recent social theorists, he has been concerned to develop a conceptualisation which addresses the various antinomies (see Chapter 2 for a discussion of these), which too-often seemed to lure previous theorists into unnecessarily one-sided views. Although Bourdieu has written several laboured theoretical tomes, the main thrust of his analytical approach is to assist empirical analyses. Theoretical work *per se* is considered to detract from the trajectory of his (or any other social analyst's) main interest as a researcher.

Since his approach is particularly 'relational', it is difficult to obtain an easy entry into his analytical system. The analysis works between collective and individually-based concepts, between the subjective and the objective and in a correspondingly mediating position in terms of the other antinomies. Key concepts include 'habitus' (the mental schemas that people employ to order their world and which shapes their actions), capital and field: although these key terms are supplemented by many others.

Any society comprises at least one, and usually several, fields. These are similar to the concept of an institutional area (e.g. religion, the family, the economy etc.), although they may be larger or smaller than these, depending on the historical development of the field itself – in particular, the extent to which it has erected strong boundaries and has acquired a high degree of autonomy. Each field consists of an array of actors (who have entered it) who take positions in relation to the struggles and competition within the field. Many fields are structured into a 'dominant fraction' and a 'dominated fraction', with the former shaping the rules governing activity within that field to lean towards their interests. It is a key part of the concept of field that it is seen as relational and in a state of dynamic tension: positions are related to others and the field is energised by on-going struggles and competition (except in the limiting, pathological case where struggle has been squelched by the setting up of an authoritative 'apparatus'). Wacquant suggests that the metaphor of a magnetic field is appropriate, although I think that the more general image of an electronic field would be more apt.

The struggles are over the 'stake' of the field, especially capturing the setting of rules within it. One important type of struggle concerns 'symbolic classification': the struggle to develop and impose particular ways of seeing the field and what is happening in it. Those whose ability to resist is weak may be the victims of 'symbolic violence' perpetrated against them, which seeks to deny their right to exist socially and undermines the legitimacy of their preferred style of operating in this field.

However, there is also a resource-base to struggles in any field. Participants each seek to mobilise the particular types of capital they have at their command in order to improve their position. Capitals that may be relevant include economic, political, cultural and social (this last being the fluid operational form of capital that involves network connections etc.). Bourdieu's approach very usefully draws on the Marxian insistence on the importance of material commodities produced in economic fields, but extends this concept to a wider range of 'resources' which are valued in social life. So, a field consists of a distribution of types of capital (the relevance of particular types of capital is set by the nature of the field involved), which are then employed in the struggles, which in turn affect the distribution of the various types of resource, and so on.

At the individual level, people's actions are seen as being shaped by their internalised 'habitus' which provides them with orientating meanings and shapes their actions – at a partially unconscious level. The habitus is laid down in childhood and is shared by broad groupings of people, but is dynamically altered to better fit changing social circumstances. The 'habitus' tends over time to become suited to the position in which the person is placed within the field, and so continues to provide a changing operating style appropriate to changing circumstances. Thus, activity at the individual level is affected by, but also affects, the operation of collective levels of social life.

Finally, Bourdieu's analytical framework is completed by a vision of the overall social structure which works behind the various fields, and which involves patterns of linkage between separate fields. While Bourdieu does not advance a universalistic theory of social structure, he does accord an important role to the generic field of 'power' in which the class structure in particular is located. This most general field continues to operate behind various of the more specific fields, and may penetrate and control these, especially where their autonomy is not strong. Often this appearance of autonomy is illusory, as a field seems to echo the patterns of the underlying, more general, field. For example, the education system (without explicit reference to the underlying more general stratificational order) acts effectively to reproduce the class structure from generation to generation. The overseeing role of the State can also be strong and effective.

There is room here for only a few evaluative comments to be made. These particularly involve the difficult presentation of much of his material, and the further development it still needs. Although Bourdieu's work is sensitive to social differences, the extent of determination exuded by 'fields' is over-emphasised and there is insufficient play of people's actions.

Giddens

In a series of theoretical works stretching from the mid-1970s, Giddens has developed the most sophisticated generally available theory of social structure, usually advanced under the banner of the theory of 'structuration' (see Giddens 1984; Archer 1982; Clark 1990). Giddens is less concerned with developing a conceptual framework, which would then allow the derivation of more specific theories, than endeavouring to recover from the available stock of social theories a vision of social structure which can be sustained philosophically.

The theory of structuration spins off from an examination of functionalism and structuralism on the one hand, with their deterministic approaches emphasising collectivities, and on the other hand from an examination of theories stressing meaningful action, with their voluntaristic approaches emphasising individuals and their agency.

A core point is an emphasis on the enabling as well as the more usually emphasised constricting aspects of social structure. Giddens has also been struck with the strategic usefulness of time-geography (which is a fine-grained investigation of the daily rounds of people over the 24-hour period and across their usual round of locales). This provides for a concrete grounding of any sociology in the details of human activity.

Human action is set between the unacknowledged grounds of action and its unintended consequences. Giddens emphasises the way human action takes the form of routinised and recursive practices of activity, together with the regular small-scale social interactions in which these are coordinated. These regular practices are in part driven by sheer habit, but are also skilled performances delivered by 'knowledgeable' actors. Much of our sense of social reality lies within the concreteness of these daily rounds of activity: they usually are able to provide the 'ontological security' we crave. These practices are seen as often comprising systems of interaction which may achieve a considerable degree of integration, and which are woven together by skilled performances.

The question then becomes, 'How are we as actors able to produce such practices?' Social structure is seen as supplying the material needed to produce such practices, but also itself is reproduced through such practices. Indeed, social structure is seen as having no existence other than that which is made to come alive (instantiated) in these practices, and which is embodied in memory traces of the mind. In particular, social structure is seen as providing the 'time-space' binding that allows practices to be projected over distances (beyond face-to-face interaction) and over time.

This ephemeral social structure, which is drawn on in conducting practices, consists of 'rules' and 'resources'. 'Rules', in a very wide sense, are seen as involving the conceptions of social order held by participants, and also moral evaluations of what social order should be. The rules provide the recipes to be followed in producing and legitimating a social practice. Allocative and authoritative resources are also put into action to produce social practices. The former refers to material resources and the latter to relations between people (e.g. power). So there is no structure apart from that which is called into being by human activity. The systems of practices may have structural properties, but they are not themselves structures. On the other hand, such structural properties may be strongly institutionalised, and there are sets of structural principles (such as the patterns constituting capitalism) which form comprehensive higher-order patterns.

Giddens is careful not to admit to too much 'materiality' of material resources. He correctly points out that, however imposing resources may be, they are nothing until invoked by human action (indeed, this is the very definition of a resource).

Human action is seen as variously steered by people operating with different mixes of the three levels of:

1 fully conscious reflexive monitoring;
2 practical action; and
3 subconscious motivations for action.

In general, social structure is produced as an unintentional by-product of more concrete types of human activity. However, under some conditions it can be consciously steered and directed.

The end result of this schema is to produce an extremely 'lean' and insubstantial version of social structure, which springs up only in micro-situations. A conceptual conjuring trick is performed: now you see it, now you don't. Giddens' account disappoints structuralists as collective entities are conjured away. On the other hand, his account seems highly philosophically correct in that it avoids positing social realities whose existence cannot be adequately theorised.

It is interesting, though, that Giddens leaves open a backdoor for more general macro-level accounts of social structure to be developed. He argues that more general images of social structure are viable, and indeed produces such analyses himself, but in other stretches of his writing. There seems to be a definite tension (as with Weber) between his more general statements of structuration theory, and some of his other writing.

My own view is that, while Giddens' views may be very difficult to refute, in practice social structure imposes itself with great force. Certainly, social structure cannot work until called into action. Similarly, the information stored in a computer is of little use until the machine is switched on and a programme is available to access the data. But once accessed such material can be very powerful. Another way of thinking about this could be the scenario of when you are asleep, social structure (at least your own contribution to it) evaporates (although sleeping arrangements are often defensive and also thoughts connected with social structure may well dance through your dreams). However, on awakening, social structure returns with full force. As you stumble through the routines of waking and rising, the memory stores are progressively mobilised, and one's place in the social structure is quickly re-established. Not only are one's memory traces imbued with a lifetime of rules and experiences, but in most societies the stock of resources forms a monumental reality. The weight of social structure is overwhelming once it is enacted. But Giddens's picture does not grasp this weightiness.

Moreover, Giddens' practices are strangely un-populated. Real people are involved with these and their pattern of social interaction is vital in securing the activity they are jointly developing. Even more so, groupings of people are involved.

On the whole, Bourdieu's schema seems rather more satisfactory sociologically. Whereas Giddens' memory traces seem quite psychological, Bourdieu's habitus is clearly not only shared across each of different groupings (e.g. classes), but is an instrument of social differentiation (in that different social groupings have different habituses): they are often complementary to each other within a wider system. Bourdieu's main drawback is that his analysis exudes a mysticism which is not carefully exorcised from his conceptual thinking.

Related debates

But not all theorising of social structure has involved the construction of a 'general theory' of social structure, as with Bourdieu and Giddens. An important, but more indirect, form which the pursuit of theories of social structure has taken involves debates focused on issues which are directly relevant to it.

Ritzer (1991) argues that the agenda of social theory in the 1980s has been focused on the micro–macro issue (which was barely raised before then). He also argues that there has been a transatlantic differentiation in the way this debate has been put forward, with Continental theorists being more concerned with the related agency–structure concern. (These debates also relate to other relevant debates, such as those over subjective–objective dualism.) In both the micro–macro and the agency–structure debates, most hold the ideal to be a reasonable balance between both ends of the continua, while some stress intermediate positions such as dialectical or interactional relations between the levels. (Collections on this debate include: Alexander 1987; Eisenstadt and Helle 1985; Fielding 1988; Gilbert 1989; Helle and Eisenstadt 1985; Huber 1991; Knorr-Cetina and Cicourel 1981, together with a host of more specialist articles or books, e.g. Fuchs 1989; Haugaard 1992; Holmwood and Stewart 1991; Lloyd 1993; Manicas 1987.)

CONTEMPORARY WORK ON SOCIAL STRUCTURE

The Array of recent work

In the wake of the structuralist writings and the theoretical work of Blau, direct sustained and systematic attention to social structure has been limited apart from the work of contemporary mathematical sociologists, and theorists such as Bourdieu and Giddens, together with the several fields of theoretical debate as noted above.

'Social structure' has nevertheless received continued but sporadic attention. In this section, I will indicate something of the range of recent developments, including books (or significant articles) by Archer (1995), Blau (1993), Burns and Flam (1987), Burt (1992), Coleman (1990), Cook and Whittmeyer (1992), Knottnerus and Prendergast (1994), Kontopolous (1993), Layder (1994), Lockwood (1992), Mouzelis (1990; 1991; 1995), Namboordi and Corwin (1993), Porpora (1987; 1989; 1993), Ridgeway (1994), Sayer and Walker (1992), Sewell (1992), Stinchcombe (1983), Sztompka (1991), Wellman and Berkowitz (1988) and White (1992), and the stream of articles being published in the *Journal for the Theory of Social Behaviour*.

Since this work constitutes the 'research front' of discussion about social structure, it can be difficult to draw out the implications of this work, let alone see how it fits together. Indeed, I will only generally indicate something of the two main directions in which recent work has been developed.

Formal analysis

By the mid-1980s, an intellectual movement of social theorists began to develop a programme of formal structural analysis. While this centred on network analysis (see Wellman and Berkowitz 1988), a broader alliance, also involving related approaches, was envisaged. Other similar approaches are those involved in exchange theory, rational choice approaches and game theory. In addition, some quantitative data-analysts have endeavoured to draw out theoretical models.

One institutional home for this movement has been a series of books with an editorial board (chaired by Mark Granovetter) consisting of a glittering array of the names of leading structural analysts. This provides an unusually concise glimpse into this approach. In his 'Series Introduction', Granovetter proclaims that the series will:

> ... present approaches that explain social behaviour and institutions by reference to relations among such concrete social entities as persons and organisations. .... The methodological core of structural analysis is the 'social network' approach but the series will also draw on a large body of work in areas such as political economy, conflict, human ecology, social psychology, organisational analysis, social mobility, sociology of science and bio-sociology, among others, that is not framed explicitly in network terms, but stresses the importance of relations rather than the atomisa-tion of reductionism or the determinism of ideas, technology or material conditions.
>
> (Granovetter 1988, Preface)

It is further claimed that the perspective 'has become extremely popular and influential in all the social sciences, [but that] it does not have a coherent identity' (1988). However, this is but one approach within a broad stream.

Exegesis and elaboration

Another major axis of interest in social structure involves various attempts to critique and to rework the formulations of Bourdieu, Giddens and other theorists, including drawing on much older traditions of thinking about society. This line of writing is much more inclined to remain embedded in detailed exegesis of texts rather than opening up to the real world. Never-theless, useful distinctions are often advanced and the sophistication of thinking about social structure slowly improves.

There are also some signs that the two camps of writing on social structure are drawing somewhat together (e.g. Knottnerus and Prendergast 1994), although, in the main, the two remain worlds apart.

The very considerable range of contemporary writing on social structure makes it difficult for it to be fully worked in with the main approaches summarised in this book. I have endeavoured to draw on it as much as possible in the next two chapters.

CONCLUSION

Beyond the particular content of successive theories of social structure, there may lie a more general path of overall development of the concept.

Employment of the concept began with general, essentially descriptive uses. It was used in practice by many social analysts, but its essential features were not explicated. In the 1930s, the concept became more refined and more contrasted with other dimensions for studying social life, especially culture. However, the sporadic efforts to forge specific, clear-cut concepts tended to quickly dissipate back again into wider usages. In the 1950s and 1960s, some systematic and complex theoretical frameworks concerning social systems were developed. However, these complex systems of ideas failed to win widespread adherence and, in the wake of their demise, the concept of social structure tended to fade in its salience for theoretical work. Recent contributions to social structural analysis are still being couched in somewhat idiosyncratic terms: arguments are put forward but few are built on a common foundation.

However, such a broad picture does not capture well the overall advance of conceptual work on social structure. Writing on this topic has been scattered, piecemeal and not particularly cumulative. Nevertheless, many lessons have been accumulated on the pitfalls of theorising social structures. And many useful pieces of the jigsaw puzzle have been constructed, and await being placed into a more general picture. The assemblage of material in this book is a modest beginning to this task.

There are a few lessons to be learned from reflecting on the history of social structural analysis:

- it seems useful to quite clearly separate social structure both from its (external) causes and its effects rather than using it as a global category encompassing everything;
- as well as seeking understanding of how a social structure operates, it is important to ground this understanding in the on-going everyday life of members;
- it is also important to contextualise the social structure in terms of its long-term tendencies, and its relations with other social structures;
- particular care is needed to link micro (e.g. 'the interactional order') and macro aspects of social structures, and it is particularly important to capture both the determined (structure) and the voluntaristic (agency) aspects of social life;
- finally, another distinction which may be helpful is the one between the ideas and meanings involved with culture and the interactions and resource-

flows involved with social structure, which certainly must always be addressed.

This chapter has highlighted the challenge of the task of trying to 'pack down' the literature on social structure. The history of the development of the term illustrates very clearly the huge diversity of views on social structure. It is to this challenge of providing a conceptual order, other than a merely chronological one, that the next two chapters are addressed.

4

THEORETICAL ISSUES RELATING TO SOCIAL STRUCTURE

ISSUES IN ANALYSING SOCIAL STRUCTURES

The historical treatment (in Chapter 3) has revealed many of the quite different approaches to social structure which are available. It is now appropriate to consolidate this material. In doing this, we need to separate out two quite different areas of debate concerning social structure. On the one hand there are questions relating to the *nature* of social structures and, on the other, questions about the *scope* of social structures.

Debates about the nature of social structure concern more philosophical issues and are discussed in this chapter. Debates about the scope of different types of social structures bear more on sociology as a discipline trying to describe and understand the world, and are discussed in Chapter 5. Debates about the nature and scope are not sealed off from each other, so that material from the two chapters interpenetrates, but it is useful to try to treat each separately – at least to begin with.

Debates about the nature of any phenomenon in turn break down into concerns about ontology and epistemology: what the phenomenon is and how it might be revealed to us and studied. Epistemological discussions often revolve around what a scientific, humanistic or other approach to social reality might involve, and therefore how sociology as a science might proceed. This topic was raised in the introductory chapter and is considered again here, but clearly has a much wider scope and can be only touched on in this book, even though it keeps on returning to haunt us. The ontological issue is rather more immediately central, as fierce and highly pertinent debates rage around the extent to which there is a collective reality beyond the persons involved with a social structure.

Accordingly, the first two sections summarise some of the arguments about the nature of social reality. The following six sections each examine social structure from the perspective of a particular philosophical viewpoint. Each of these viewpoints has a sharp challenge to pose, and an adequate understanding of social structure has to be able to sufficiently answer these challenges. The main sections in the rest of this chapter will be examining the following themes:

- social structure is seen by structuralists as operating without people in it;
- social structure is seen by critical realists as riven by hidden pressures which can be explosive;
- social structure is seen by individualists as only involving the people within it;
- social structure is seen by ethologists as quite common across a wide range of species;
- social structure is seen by culturalists as merely an expression of the culture;
- social structure is seen by postmodernists as a diffuse and unordered mosaic of local occurrences.

The final section of this chapter attempts to summarise some of the responses to these challenges by sketching a model of social structure which gives a good purchase on its essential characteristics while avoiding some of the more obvious points of criticism.

ARGUMENTS FOR A STRUCTURAL LEVEL OF ANALYSIS

The power of a social structural approach comes from its basic premise that people's attributes, attitudes and behaviour (what they have, what they think and what they do) arises (in an appreciable part) from their position in the social structure; and further, that particular structural arrangements – the way things are organised – will differ in their social effects.

As Blau and Merton (1981) argued, sociology has a common concern with 'emergent effects'. But it is important that these be specified. Moreover, the argument for emergence must be tested against the 'null hypotheses' that either there is no social regularity at all (the strong version) or that the apparent structuredness of social life arises purely from chance (the weak version).

Callinicos (1987) gives the following anti-reductionist arguments concerning the structural autonomy of social structures:

1 they have a degree of 'systemness' and interdependence (further, there are limits to their variability without becoming a different kind of social structure);
2 they persist over time, especially over generations of members;
3 structures are a set of (empty) places not dependent on the identities of the particular people filling them.

In these ways, structures pre-exist any particular individual and they also continue after particular individuals have left them. This rather basic list can be extended by further arguments about the structural level of social life:

4 aggregation – often people do similar things as a result of similar conditions, and therefore there is a definite appearance of things being done in common (a more prosaic example is the way that yachts at anchor each swing in a similar direction to face the general direction of the tide);

61

5 such similarity may be further reinforced when people notice that things are being done in common, which encourages them to decide to follow suit ('contagion' or other forms of aggregate social psychology);

6 structures are mainly experienced as hard and factual, external to the individual and with a 'coercive force' which is sometimes quite direct, as in the application of direct physical force;

7 the existing prior gathering of people and social organisations has an effect in itself, since it provides the context against which people react and shapes their opportunities;

8 structures are biologically, and perhaps psychologically, required because of the long periods of biological dependence of the young, old and sick; because cooperation seems often necessary to sustain a livelihood from nature; and also because of the apparent need by humans for social interaction to retain their sanity and sense of 'ontological security';

9 social structures (at least in the broadest terms) are common across species;

10 agents involved in them are not always aware of the regularities, let alone understand them, and yet the structures continue to work 'behind their backs' irrespective of their consciousness or wilful involvement;

11 people impinge on each other because of the mutual interdependence of their decisions: opportunities for one are often thereby denied others (these are zero-sum games);

12 as the concept of 'life-chances' points up, groupings of people share important aspects of their fate (events sometimes affect groupings collectively);

13 there is a limited ability for any individual to change his/her environing structures (despite the partly contrary doctrines such as the 'great man theory of history' or the idea of 'charismatic leaders');

14 agents can choose (rationally or not) to bind themselves into collectivities through some form of 'social contract';

It is surprising that this 'case for structure' is not apparently easily available and well-rehearsed by sociologists. (While I have merely assembled various arguments which circulate in the sociological literature, this is useful as I know of no accounts where an agenda of such points is brought together.) Some of the points deserve some immediate commentary.

• the contagion or similarity effect noted as point 5 is often taken by analysts to be insufficiently structural to really 'count' as a properly collectivist explanation;

• the classic case made by Durkheim has been summarised here as point 6;

• the biological and psychological reason for the formation of structure is a 'functionalist one', which would need to be recast in order to meet objections against this form of explanation. However, it is not difficult to sense that there could be a general 'pressure' for some development of social forms as a result of biological or psychological needs of individuals, even if this pressure did not lead to particular social forms being developed;

- the second to last point is taken to be a summary one which pools the effects of the others, and repeats at an individualistic level the more general first point made by Callinicos. Many sociologists would accept some validity for 'great men of history' or 'charismatic leadership' arguments. However, their rarity (which can be taken as reasonable) is evidence of the durable effects of structures. In any case, sociologists would argue that such individual effects only operate under specific social conditions;
- the last point is the central argument of the rational choice theorists.

It is possible that this listing could be tidied up by collapsing elements, by better organising, or even by an identification of the contradictions which might arise if several were held simultaneously. Indeed, I think that the above arguments can be assembled into five different ways in which people can have an involvement with social structures. (This is a 'stratification' schema of involvement.)

1 People may only *apparently* be acting socially.
2 People may 'carry' social structure through the unintended (or intended) consequences of their actions, irrespective of their knowledge or will.
3 People may 'adjust' their own behaviour to that of other *individuals*.
4 People may 'adjust' their own behaviour to that of social *collectives*.
5 People may *choose* to pledge themselves to be bound by social collectivities.

This forms a hierarchy of involvement with social arrangements. In any situation we need to be sensitive to the level of social bonding involving the participants.

ONTOLOGICAL ISSUES: WHAT IS THE NATURE OF THE BEAST?

Views on social structure have ontological implications. It is all very well to postulate a collective social structure beyond the individuals composing it, but what reality does this entity have? Such problems afflict many other areas of scientific work too. Often grasping the reality of a phenomenon is reliant on scientific instrumentation, which in turn is based in theoretical schemata. Sometimes, the reality of a social phenomenon can be grasped only through its visible effects: e.g. the poetic image of a wind only being seen as it sweeps across a wheat-field or blusters trees on a ridge.

A preliminary point of view to consider concerns the dividing line between 'science' and 'philosophy'. It can be reasonably argued that the ontological status of concepts which scientists use is really a matter to be passed over to philosophers to be concerned about. As far as the scientist is concerned it is a 'catch as catch can' situation, and they can be quite free to postulate whatever entities they like as long as this proves explanatorily useful. On the other hand, in dealing with social phenomena (given the moral connotations this implies), it behoves the social scientist to be careful with the concepts that are being used. A compromise would be to attend to ontological issues, but not at the expense of being significantly diverted by them.

Another aspect of this issue is to consider the relationship between the models of social reality that we, as observers, may conjure up, and what is 'out there'. Lévi-Strauss was most emphatic on this point, saying that his models were very much only in the observer's head (see Chapter 3). Most, though, feel that while their models are in their heads, they reflect structural aspects of actual social reality out there (however difficult it may be to establish this link).

Few would push their belief in the existence of structures to exclude a role for people. However, some doctrines minimise this role and cast people as quite 'dopey' and involved only as 'bearers' of the structure. The opposite position is 'radical individualism' in which every proposition must, at least in principle, be reduced to individual terms. Another position (e.g. advocated by Coleman 1990) is that, under certain conditions, a group of individuals can so bind themselves together that they form an entity operating much as a single person would. Examples of this include formally-constituted groups but also mobs. From this position, collective properties can be posited while emphasising their bases in individual action.

Another commonly held position is that, through social processes, what is inherently subjective and ephemeral can be built into something which is experienced as, and held to be, objective and factual (e.g. see Berger and Luckman 1966; also discussed in Chapter 3). In this, social structures become a 'third world' hovering somewhere between the objective world of facts and the subjective world of 'imaginaries'. In this approach, structures are real in their effects, only in so far as they are 'socially constructed'. But after all, the common-sense view of concrete reality that we draw from our experience does not stand up to the scrutiny of a physicist: the common-sense reality of tables and chairs dissipates into a cloud of atoms (and, in turn, these have been found to be decomposable still further). So maybe we merely need to shift our views on what 'reality' involves.

From the viewpoint of the victim, social forces can often seem extremely real. Being carted off by the police might be one example of the reality behind the 'majesty of the law'. But from the viewpoint of the police, their enforcement is certainly something which is socially constructed: as the classic question phrases it: Who will guard the guardians? In sociological explanations, the existence of some hard social reality can never be assumed: rather, the sociologist always has to show how that reality came to be constructed. On the other hand, the phrase 'socially constructed' needs to be carefully considered. Not just any social facts are socially constructed. There are not endless phantom police presences hovering out there at the imaginative whim of an observer.

Only some of the potential range of realities which might be conjured up have a potent force.

In sum, there are four main stances on the ontological status of social structures which can be taken. These are subdivided by the main weight of emphasis on an individual as opposed to a collective level, and then on whether this emphasis is insisted on exclusively (the 'radical' posture) or whether it is more tentative (the 'methodological' posture).

Table 4.1 Positions on ontological status

	Main emphasis	
Strategy	*Individual*	*Collective*
Radical	R Individualist	R Collectivist
Methodological	M Individualist	M Collectivist

Table 4.1 is not that helpful, in as much as the views of most sociologists would span the lower two cells. My own suggestions are that it is useful for sociologists to be able to postulate social structures as collective entities, as these will be helpful in developing theories about structural processes and effects. However, at least in principle, there should be attempts to link these to individuals. People must have some role to play (and this is very far from saying that everything must be reducible to individuals), although they often do so through social groups composed of individuals.

This treatment of this philosophical topic is clearly inadequate. However, hopefully enough has been covered for a social structural analyst to be alerted to some of the ontological issues involved.

RELATION TO STRUCTURALISM AS AN INTELLECTUAL MOVEMENT

The development of social structural analysis has, in part, taken place within a broader movement of 'structuralism'. Structuralism has been a multi-disciplinary movement which has emphasised rational analysis of broad themes running through social life, has posited sharp breaks between surface appearances and underlying realities, and has tended to portray mere humans as epiphenomenal 'carriers' of the structures which operate behind their backs. Many of its basic ideas emanated from developments in linguistics early in the twentieth century, but it then became more specifically linked to social sciences through Lévi-Strauss in anthropology and Althusser in Marxian analysis (as I have already outlined in the section on structuralism in Chapter 3).

This broader structuralism had a beneficial effect in its advancing of theoretical and philosophical concerns and the innovative arrogance of its sweeping theories. It forced a hothouse-grown improvement of theoretical work. However, its very boldness seemed forced. As almost a direct over-reaction, it has been largely swept away by later influences which emphasise more strongly the role of actors in human events. Even its 'half-way house' successor of post-structuralism has become merged within other approaches.

The relationship between structuralism as a broad intellectual movement and the types of structural analysis covered in this book is problematic. Broadly speaking, social structural analysts have been part of a tradition which pre-dates (and post-dates) much of the most fervent development of structuralist thinking. Indeed, Lash has suggested that structuralism was retrospectively written back into the sociological record:

> When the Anglo-Saxon and sociological reception of French structural-ism was just beginning... it was rather unreflectingly assumed... the structures of the French were similar to the structural-functionalism of Parsons and Durkheim. Hence people started calling Parsons, Durkheim and the French theorists 'structuralists', given the currency of the new theoretical fashion from France. The sociologists... (mis)understood French structuralism in terms of the social structures... [and] fully missed the entire linguistic turn of the French theory.
>
> (Lash 1990: x)

However, any such conflation was only superficial. In fact, there has long been a difficult relationship between the more empirical senses of structuralism (e.g. the SAS described in Chapter 3) and the broader structuralism of the 1960s:

- part of this strain is spatial or, rather, cultural: the distinction between Anglo-American 'empiricism' and Continental 'rationalism';
- part has been a temporal disjuncture, with the full-blown development of structuralism following after the more empirical version was already well-advanced;
- part has been the relative emphasis on *social* structure as opposed to *cultural* structure.

The boundary has been marked by some abrupt exchanges, such as those between Radcliffe-Brown and Lévi-Strauss (see Lévi-Strauss 1952). More frequently there has been short sharp disavowal without much understanding (e.g. Blau 1975).

The relation between structuralism in general and social structural ap-proaches in sociology in particular is that they share some similarities in the importance they accord theory and the collective level of social life. But there are also definite differences, with sociologists not holding to the strong philosophical assumptions of the structuralists, and wishing to relate their theories more closely to empirical reality.

THE DEPTH DYNAMICS OF SOCIAL STRUCTURES

Another approach is to take the concept of structures – in the plural – more seriously. Were such creatures to be posited, how might they operate? And how might they best be studied? Some interpretations of Marx, and especially those refracted through a 'realist' philosophy of science, which posits underlying realities as opposed to surface appearances, provide an appropriate conceptualisation for such an approach (see Bhaskar 1979; Keat and Urry 1975; Sayer 1991).

One of the most important lessons we should draw from Marx (continuing the treatment in Chapter 3) is how social structures are to be studied. (I think that as well as that, Marx provided superb insights into the fundamental nature of capitalism – even if aspects of his analysis remain problematic – but that is not the point I wish to debate here. I also recognise that the lessons I am endeavouring to extract from Marx's work might well be disputed by many, but it is not relevant to defend my viewpoint here.)

Marx provided a structuralist analysis of the operation and development of capitalism. First, he was able to specify the preconditions for the development of capitalism and then to show that, historically, these were present. (This is much the same line of argument that biologists take when they point out that biological life was sparked off amid the primordial chemical soup once the right array of ingredients had assembled itself). He then had an operational model of how capitalism itself worked, through the relationship between the two key structural groupings of owners and workers. This relationship has a simple core involving exploitation of the proletariat's labour-power by the bourgeoisie, although Marx is also able to provide a more rich and highly ramified understanding of the complexities of this relationship. The third key aspect of this model is that it identifies an immanent tendency within capitalism to expand, given the insatiable need of the system to develop ever-expanding markets. This, in turn, leads to an understanding of the external constraints that may limit the growth of capitalism. (An alternative way of putting this is to see these as capitalism outrunning the limitations imposed by its underlying conditions – which may be related to, but can be quite different from, the preconditions that allowed it to develop in the first place.)

Finally, Marx's model is able to show that, within itself, Capitalism can breed the seeds of its own destruction as a system. As the structure becomes more and more polarised, internal opposition is built up, and it can collapse into a series of ever-deepening crises which finally may lead to the rise of another type of social structure from its ashes. Marx's model of capitalism illustrates well the key features any model of the development of a 'structure' must cover.

One important point is the distinction between the capitalist structure (in Marx's terms a 'mode of production') and the wider social order (in Marx's terms

67

a 'social formation') of which the dominant mode is but one part. This, in turn, opens issues about the ways different modes which sit side-by-side in a social formation may relate to each other. (Marx's answer tends to be that economic structures other than the one which is dominant will tend to be chewed up and collapse into the dominant mode.) This distinction can also open the possibility of identifying other structures which operate within the social formation, albeit in 'regions' of society other than economic production. This may even be implied by the distinction between the 'infrastructure' of the mode of (economic) production and various aspects of the 'superstructure', such as politics, religion and the family.

But what may present itself to analysts of modern societies as a surfeit of possible structures which may be at work, provides precisely the opposite problem for analysts of less technologically advanced societies, where there is often but a single, kin-based structure to carry out all the various tasks of that society. (This question has generated much debate among anthropologists and sociologists, with the main answer being that there is no reason at all why structures should not be multi-task or configured in the same way as capitalist social formations.)

What are other possible candidates of structures which can be modelled in a rigorous Marxian fashion? Certainly one may well be that of the family-cum-household, which is often organised along patriarchal lines and can be seen as being encompassed within a mode of reproduction. Another quite clear-cut structure is that of the bureaucratic state apparatus, as analysed by Weber. Beyond these obvious examples, it can be difficult to be clear about what constitutes a clear-cut structure with its own, separate inner logic of development.

What can be extracted from this exegesis of a Marxian style of analysis is a template of how a social structural explanation might be constructed. Not only must the model identify the crucial mechanisms which are involved with the operation of the structure, but it must specify how the structure was able to develop in the first place, and what its internal trends might lead to in the longer-term. And it must do all this while remaining connected up to much of the social complexities and subtleties of human life. This is, to say the very least, a very tall order. Nevertheless, it provides one standard against which the adequacy of analyses of social structures can be judged.

The work on the nature and scope of social structures which is reviewed in this book (especially in the following chapter) provides tools for grasping the various complexities of social life. It does not, however, show how the findings generated by this array of conceptual tools might readily be assembled into structural accounts of the Marxian order of powerfulness. This topic needs further work. Nevertheless, I repeat my exhortation that this is a good model of explanation to grasp, even if it seems beyond our easy reach.

THE INDIVIDUAL LEVEL

One of the key oppositional cleavages between structuralist approaches and others is in terms of the role they give the individual. Rational choice modellers and others who begin with individual level understandings are seen by structuralists as the enemy.

One reason for opposition is essentially heuristic, or at least methodological. Were analysts to over-emphasise the individual level, they might be diverted from ever studying 'emergent effects'. Similarly, many would recognise that, while in principle they are making assumptions about the psychology involved with their (implicit) 'model of man', they just do not wish to spell this out. However, some actively denigrate such models and endeavour to outlaw them from sociological consideration. This is sometimes argued on quite ideological grounds, since these individualistic approaches are seen as inflicting an implicit conservatism which denies not just social structures, but also the bad effects they often produce.

Major theoretical advances in this border-land area between sociology and psychology have been made by explicitly considering the 'image of man' involved. For example, Giddens has made a major point of emphasising the 'knowledgeability' of actors as opposed to seeing them as 'cultural dopes', and this has reshaped considerations about social structure.

Another area of important development is in the sociology of the emotions, and more recently the sociology of bodies. The neglect of these topics during past regimes of sociology is one reason leading to the current focusing of interest in social selves and identities, as well as the links between these topics and bodies.

Other sociologists are actively endeavouring to build a sociology from the bottom up. There is an emerging alliance between exchange theorists and network analysts, and more generally with rational choice modellers. Various models are developed that indicate people's motivations and actions that might lead to them combining with others. For example, Coleman argues that people will 'buy into' sharing norms with others, as it becomes in their individual interests to do so. Hechter (1990), too, is concerned with building up models of social structure on individualistic grounds, but recognises the major difficulties of doing so without accepting arguments which presuppose existing social structures: both values and resources seem almost inevitably to be obtained from outside the realm in which individuals operate. While Hechter agrees that models showing the effects of social structure are well-established, he is concerned that individualist explanations of the genesis of social structure are required. And this is by far the bigger challenge. It may be, however, that these severe difficulties fatally undermine the radical individualistic strategy.

This type of social theorising has several good points. Clear, explicit theoretical models are developed, with stated assumptions and occasionally mathematisation. These spell out assumptions about why people might be doing things, which is a topic many other sociologies leave murky. The longer-term consequences of people making particular sets of decisions can be followed through.

Drawbacks are that the situations postulated are often limited and unreal, based on speculative assumption rather than empirical data, and with doubtful relevance to the real world. Often simplistic models impose an unnecessary averaging uniformity which detracts from the considerable variability of human actions. More concerning is the fact that rational choice theorists often smuggle in collective assumptions without realising this. For example, value preferences, resource endowments or societal rules are often ignored in analyses (through being taken for granted), whereas in fact they are clearly given by social structural arrangements.

A rather different approach in sociology has been to complement the traditional emphasis on rationality, by inclusion of the emotional side of human activity. After all, emotions are a major source of energy which can infuse social structures.

Even if individual-level type models can never by themselves cover the full gamut of sociology, they are extremely important portions of every sociologists' conceptual armament. But sociologists must be aware of the social conditions under which particular models hold.

LESSONS FROM CROSS-SPECIES STRUCTURAL ANALYSES

Another argument, relating to culture, pertains to the cross-species nature of social structures. In primate (let alone other species) societies, cultural communication is minimal, without a general-purpose language. Thus, primate (and other animal) social structures might usefully test out ideas about the role of social structure in relation to culture.

Nevertheless, there are clear-cut social structures ordered around particular 'concerns' – especially territoriality and dominance. It is hardly appropriate to review the social side of ethology here, but we can at least briefly raise useful questions. Let us begin with a standard account of one type of primate social structure.

A typical savanna baboon troop has an average of forty members. How the troop organises itself can be seen in its spatial arrangements both at rest and on the move, more typically the latter. The group moves about all day foraging for food, mostly grass – and each member fends for himself. At the center of the group are the dominant males – never more than about six adults, however large the troop. Around them cluster the females and the young. Spread out around this central core are the 'cadets' – the more junior males who are candidates for the central hierarchy. The peripheral males are confined to the edges of the group; here those animals which have left their mothers and moved to the borders are joined by some older males that have not made the central hierarchy. The males of the central core act as bosses, defenders, policemen, and leaders in a complex set of actions and interactions.

(Tiger and Fox 1971: 28 ff.)

Tiger and Fox summarise common underlying features of primate social structure, despite considerable variety in species–specific surface patterns, as follows:

- The system is based on hierarchy and competition for status, which determine access to resources and the privilege of breeding.
- The males dominate the political system, and the older males dominate the younger.
- Females can be influential in sending males up the status ladder; and their long-term relationships to one another are critical for the stability of the system.
- The dominant males keep order among the females and juveniles; they are nurturers and protectors of the young.
- Cooperation among males is essential; coalitions of bonded males act as units in the dominance system.
- The whole structure is held together by the attractiveness of the dominants and the attention which is constantly paid them.
    Because of this, charismatic individuals can upset the hierarchical structure, and by the same token, retain power.

(Tiger and Fox 1971: 31–2)

There are clearly several continuities between human and primate social structures, with each operating to meet collective needs through a relatively stable division of labour, which can adjust to changing needs but which is also driven by an internal logic of its own. It is this internal logic which differs somewhat between various human social structures and the primate example given. Human societies are not quite so directly driven by 'nature red in tooth and claw', but unleash logics of their own. Another lesson is that social structures can clearly operate without much development of culture. Being able to relate social structural analysis to this 'minimalist' cross-species baseline situation is useful. Certainly, I think one of the tests for any schema of social structural analysis must be its applicability to the study of primate and other animal and insect social structures.

CULTURE VS. SOCIAL STRUCTURE

Few theorists (however, see Archer 1988; Hays 1994; Porpora 1993) have developed a particularly effective distinction between culture (or content) and social structure (or form). And irrespective of whether or not, or exactly how,

71

such a distinction can be maintained, social theorists have differed in the importance they accord this distinction. Standard textbook treatments used to refer to each as the other side of the coin to the other. On reflection, this is not particularly helpful, as it does not allow the two to be prised apart and each related to the other.

Perhaps a generally understood position is as follows. Whereas social structure refers to the (form of) relationships among social groupings composed of people, culture indicates the details and content of such relationships and of the social structure more generally, as well as other cultural material (quite separate from, or inconsequential to, social structure). The distinction is not unlike that between bodies and clothes.

Exploring this distinction further, it can be seen that there are different implications of each. Explanatory principles are different. Social structures involve the jostle of people and groupings in which there can be 'causal effects' of one grouping on another. Culture is the realm of meaning, which can be rendered down through analysis into basic underlying principles or themes which illuminate aspects of the culture. But showing how components of a culture (such as ideas) can be manifestations of themes or principles provides understanding, not causal explanation. Social structure is largely about doing and having, culture about thinking and feeling. Each social structure is unique because it operates with particular people in a particular setting and timing, although social structures can be *similar* to each other. Culture can be *common* and several different social structures could relate to (as many copies of) the same cultural pattern. Another possibility is that a social structure might change the culture it operates with, while remaining recognisable as the same social structure.

An important argument is that a 'natural science' of social structure is possible in ways that an analysis of culture could never aspire to. The argument runs as follows. Broadly, humans tend to be purposive and rational, and given that the range of types of human organisations is limited, it is likely that very similar structural arrangements will be repeatedly developed across many situations. Similar responses to similar stimuli may also be assisted by diffusion of solutions.

Simmel's concept of 'forms' (quoted in Chapter 3) is an early statement of this view. Similarly, Radcliffe-Brown argued more directly to this distinction:

> You cannot have a science of culture. You can study culture only as a characteristic of a social system. . . . if you study culture, you are always studying the acts of behaviour of a specific set of persons who are linked together in a social structure.
>
> (Simmel in Kuper 1983: 55)

In sum, culture has a plenitude of different types of form, whereas social structure is more restricted in its range. This makes it more possible to derive 'scientific laws' about the operation of social structure, whereas there is much more opportunity to trace historical links among cultural elements.

How should the two concepts be related to each other? There are several alternative stances ranging from radical structuralism to radical culturalism. The radical structuralist view (e.g. Mayhew, Blau) rejecting the influence of culture surely must itself be rejected, as it can easily be shown that such structuralists necessarily import assumptions about culture in order for their analyses to proceed. Indeed, it is quite impossible to understand a social structure without examining the 'ideas' which are its essential framework. Similarly, those unable to penetrate behind cultural forms to the social order 'carrying them' are under-analysing their data. It seems to me that both perspectives are needed in any analysis, and that neither can be reduced to the other. (As a personal preference, because of my own interest in social structure, I choose to emphasise this aspect, but I cannot ignore culture, even if I often de-emphasise it.)

Work on this distinction will be advanced by a search for instances in which differences between culture and social structure in terms of their explanatory value can be clearly identified: strategic research sites where the force of one rather than the other is more obvious.

There have been several suggestions about the conditions under which the relative strengths of culture and social structure differ. One is a critique of the 'dominant ideology thesis' (Abercrombie *et al.* 1980) in which it is argued that, as opposed to some Marxian and many culturological interpretations, modern societies are not securely integrated by an overwhelming dominant culture. Instead, the organisation of capitalism is congruent with a range of cultural frames, and many of these need provide only a quite tangential defence of the social arrangements.

Similarly, Geertz argues that the relation between economic structure and cultural superstructure is more complex than that suggested in some Marxian models. In this model, it is suggested that the superstructure lags in any change to fit with new circumstances only after infrastructural change has already happened. The growing tension, it is suggested, is not resolved by the cataclysmic total overthrow of the old. Instead, it is suggested 'the two continually grind away at each other, producing the restless movement that is perennially productive of change. Contradictions constantly arise in all areas of life and are just as steadily neutralised by their merger into something new' (Murphy 1972: 225 ff.).

Murphy also points out that some societies can continue over long periods despite 'very great contradictions' between cultural and structural arrangements. He mentions Tuaregs and Arabs. For example, the Tuareg culture proscribes a neat division into endogamous and exogamous portions: but this is not, in fact, a requirement, which gives Tuareg suitors a wide range of choice.

Culture has tended to suffer from less attention in periods of major development of sociology, although it now enjoys a surfeit of attention with the latest swing towards cultural studies. Undoubtedly, the study of social structures will come to fruition as a by-product of the increasing sophistication of cultural analyses.

THE DEATH OF THE SOCIAL

Despite the partial collapse of the conceptual centre of sociology, sociology must come to terms with a more insidious doctrine, which undermines still further social structural analysis as an approach. The considerable 'postmodernist turn' which social theory has been going through includes a strong diminution of the salience of the effects of 'social structures' (see Baudrillard 1983; Bogard 1990; Callinicos 1989; Donzelot 1988; Smart 1990; Touraine 1984).

The stronger version of postmodernist arguments can be that people's choices are so socially unconstrained that they are located merely in a 'statistical mass' devoid of social control (although the extent of cultural control through media and cultural images can be overwhelming). The weaker version of this argument posits that the hold of modern traditional social structures has loosened and that people's choices have widened, and as a result the standard verities of sociology no longer hold.

There is clearly some truth in these viewpoints and they deserve to be treated seriously. Sociologists can take several stances in relation to postmodernism. One approach is to structurally analyse the postmodernist approach itself using a dismissive sociology of knowledge. The viewpoint seems particularly attuned to those occupying relatively privileged positions in the social structure.

It is also possible that the viewpoint adopted by postmodernist analysts suffers from at least one flaw, in that it may fail to probe levels of social life in which orderliness continues to flourish. For example, Ingram criticises postmodernist analysts: 'they neglect to situate surface phenomena indicative of actual fragmentation against the background of a distorted life-world whose ideal presuppositions, when understood from the perspective of the actor, rather than the scientific observer, include solidarity and wholeness' (Ingram, cited in Gurnah and Scott 1992: 11n). In other words, if you do not look for order, you may very well not find it.

A particularly appropriate response of sociologists should be the endeavour to turn the somewhat free-floating ideas of postmodernist commentators into 'hypotheses' and to attempt to empirically validate these. In particular, the 'before' (modernist social conditions) and 'after' (postmodern conditions) must be placed within a common framework so that they might be compared. If it is posited that the social bonds holding society have loosened, or changed, it is surely important to research this to reveal the extent to which this has actually happened.

One interesting potential in postmodernist analysis that has not been developed is that this approach might be exciting precisely because it explores the 'limiting case' (i.e. extreme situation) where there is minimalist social interaction and co-presence. To what extent can a social structure be decorticated? For example, what might the social structure be of a grouping in which individuals lived alone, linked only through sophisticated and highly enabling computer technology? In this, it complements the relevance of the study of primate social structures which take the limiting case of situations where there is little development of culture.

As well as generating useful ideas for testing, postmodernist writers can provide useful critiques of existing stocks of social knowledge – it provides a different perspective. Postmodernist writers have also critiqued existing conceptions with considerable effect and it is no longer possible to write sociology as innocently as before its advent.

The 'end of the social' argument tends to be painted in too brilliant hues. Indeed, its death has been much exaggerated. This can then lead to the sort of knee-jerk defensiveness which limited the impact on sociology of structuralist thinking two decades ago. Instead, postmodernist commentaries can be seen as a useful source of ideas for propelling forward structural analyses.

A SKETCH OF SOCIAL STRUCTURE

In the penultimate section of this chapter on the nature of social structures, I would like to sketch my own distillation of an approach which attempts to meet the above theoretical issues. The image of social structure that I put forward in this section can be seen as a framework which stands behind and holds together the range of component views of social structure which I present in the next chapter.

Everyday life

Any adequate approach to understanding social life has to encompass both the everyday life in which we participate, the wider social structures which shape this everyday life, and the connections between them.

Social science explanations need, ultimately, to be grounded in the flow and flux of the routine practices of everyday life. Humans participate in endlessly repeated, yet varied, daily activities in which groupings of people as social identities, with bodies and in the setting of an actual physical environment which includes (humanly useful) resources located in real space and real time, act and interact. People's involvement in this flow of every day life can be observed and recorded, although an understanding of their cultural context will be required to interpret their actions. Involvement in the everyday flow of life is important to most people, and from that they gain their sense of concrete reality (and 'ontological security').

The activities incorporated in the flow of everyday life can be classified in a multitude of different ways. In principle, at least, social scientists can record almost all of this (although the placing of the requisite video-cameras might prove difficult, not to mention obtrusive!), but any such recording of even tiny slices of a few people's lives would quickly bog down in the mass of detail.

While the central image is the immense flux and apparent chaos of social life, we should not over-emphasise the fluidity. Much of social life involves frequently repeated routines. Moreover, such routines are regularly built into broader patterns. In and through the routines of daily life, stocks of resources are built up. People acquire access to, or ownership of, stocks of capital or resources. It may not always be possible to access these readily or immediately, but often the mobilisation of considerable stocks of resources can take place.

We need to apprise these complexities of the everyday world through appropriate analytical concepts. One important analytical layering to the flow of social life can be identified by drawing on Merton's classic paradigm of 'orientations' to classify each type of involvement in everyday life as:

- routine;
- ritualistic adherence;
- anomic withdrawal; or
- innovative change.

If much of the round of activities can be put into the 'routine' categorisation, this should be an indication that a 'normal' state of things pertains. Other mixes will show that situations may have different 'tones', in terms of the degree of commitment to the situation exhibited by people involved with it.

Decision-making at the core

At a less abstract level, we can look at the social involvement of each person through the prism of their constant decision-making – their control over their own activities (see Stinchcombe 1975). This is because the everyday round is produced first through the stream of decision-making that people make, and then their actions to implement the decisions they have made. Implementation, of course, involves acting on goals, mobilising resources, and manoeuvring within the interaction order within which the everyday world is framed.

At base, people's decisions at any time tend to imply one of the above four orientations, although social analysis usually focuses on rather more substantive aspects of content than these. Where possible, more strategically important decisions should be looked at, as these will reveal more about social life. To understand anyone's decision-making, the analyst must know something of the opportunities to make decisions, goals, information, costs and benefits, available resources, interaction-contacts, and decision-making style. People are often very aware of the costs of making (rational) decisions and will often therefore make their decisions on the most *ad hoc* and incremental basis. Both Giddens and Bourdieu have drawn attention to this in their models of 'decision-making' – Bourdieu's notion of 'habitus' as the semi-conscious decision-making matrix conveys this, and Giddens provides three different levels of conscious involvement in the decisions. Casting this point in terms of 'decision-making' is not entirely repeating these two formulations because my terminology is designed to draw specific attention to the (highly variable) aspect of 'choice'. People do not just participate in the everyday round of life; their participation is studded with a socially shaped and endless range of possible choices, about which they make (or don't make) their (socially shaped) decisions.

A related image from which to view people's social participation is to see them as involved with 'games'. Several analysts (including Crozier and Burrawoy) have used this approach to good effect. The metaphor of a game picks up the rule-bound nature of many situations, but also shows the dynamic and interactive aspects.

> The rules of chess are very stable, and they are imposed on each game by a convention external to that game, a convention which is a kind of absolute and extraneous datum as far as any one game is concerned. The account of the origin of that convention and the processes by which it is sustained, is in no way part of the analysis of an individual game. Not so for the sociologist. The tacit rules or constraints limiting human behaviour are not stable, and the mechanisms which enforce them are not extraneous to the story in progress: on the contrary, from the sociologist's viewpoint they are by far the most interesting aspect of that game. The constraints, the 'rules' within which social life is played out, are themselves a consequence of the game. A 'structural' account of a society is an account of how this comes to be; how the game itself generates and sustains the limits within which it is played.
>
> (Gellner 1973: 122)

The social scientists' task, then, can be seen as understanding the patterns of decisions that people make. One way of proceeding from this point is to examine lots of decisions made by lots of separate people. However, this is undoubtedly a difficult explanatory route to follow because it is unlikely that individual activity or decision-making can be completely broken down into individual units. Attention instead has also to be addressed to the activities and decisions of groups of people. There are (at least) four arguments to support this:

1 Since similar people take similar actions in similar situations (and it is common for people to be similar to others and in similar situations), it is more 'economical' for the social analyst to group individuals.
2 Some of the activities of the individuals are 'banded together' by a combined commitment to do something together (so that the grouping thus formed can be seen pretty much as a single operating unit).

3 Some of the possessions of the group can be seen as collective possessions of it (e.g. 'public goods') which cannot be individually assigned.
4 There is interplay and inter-action within the 'field' of the grouping: the actions of one arise in reaction to the actions of another, often in dynamic interplay.

The structural level

Therefore, although the first of these arguments is really pragmatic rather than analytical, they conjoin to press the case for analysis at the structural level. Although individuals have an essential role in social structures, not all aspects of social structures can be completely reduced to the individual level. In sum, we understand the decisions of an individual by understanding his or her position in the social structure.

This, in turn, can mean that we explain someone's actions in terms of their structural position and the resources made available to someone in that position: their goals, opportunities etc. Resources available to a person can include a variety of the several types of capital that Bourdieu has identified: economic, cultural and social.

Does this mean that social structures have a reality of their own? Social structures are not alive and able to be decision-making like the individuals involved with them, but they certainly have their own reality. While individuals are essential in the operation of any social structure, the involvement of individuals may not be as crucial to what happens as the central thrust of the social structure which may be at work (at least partially) behind their backs.

One key point about social structures is that they should usually be seen in the plural. There are many social structures involved in any more-or-less autonomous society. Social structures can operate at different scales and therefore can be nested within each other or cut across each other.

Production-systems

A structure is always a social grouping of individuals (and other social entities) linked by different types of relationships, which is involved with the processing of some product, together with reproduction and maintenance of itself. Relationships among the component units may vary considerably. One way of depicting them is in terms of a continuum which stretches from cooperation, through competition, to conflict. The processing of a product usually requires an input of resources, and may involve production of new resources and/or the distribution of existing resources.

Products need not be material commodities at all, but can also comprise cultural material or even social capital (as Bourdieu indicates). Almost all social structures are involved with the production of a range of resources, although many may concentrate on a particular type. Finally, reproduction may also cover various degrees of change (from development and imperialistic drive through to decline and extinction).

Following Marx, it would seem a reasonable hypothesis to suggest that the key to understanding the way in which a social structure is organised lies in the way its production process is organised. This involves the distribution of power and ownership of the resources required to make the product. However, this is easier said than done. This criterion may also be useful in sorting out the boundaries which separate different social structures from each other.

This way of considering the productive and the coordinating aspects of social structures echoes Bales' distinction between instrumental and expressive activities or leadership (also reflected in Parsons' AGIL scheme). The same idea is expressed in Durkheimian sociology in terms of the relationship between the division of labour and social integration.

In the frame of the classic subjective–objective dichotomy, social structures are a considerable mix. They are socially constructed and maintained through a variety of classificatory and symbolic processes, which tend to constitute the social structure as 'real' to its participants. Around this core of constructed positions, and relations among them, are several social processes:

- the assigning of people to, and the movement of people among, positions;
- the flows of resources and energy;
- the web of social relationships and exchanges.

Social structures are multi-stranded complexes of processes which defy easy categorisation into either objective or subjective categories. Although many obtain high durability and force, they are in fact constructed through daily accretions, through a myriad of social processes which can be subject to considerable variability and change.

Team sports as an example

Two key points are that social structures 'do' things, and they also must make sure that they hang together. An illustration of a social structure is any team sport. Any collective sport involves competition between several teams (often two). Each team is controlled by the overall rules and goals for the game which the two teams share and which are enforced by referees, and there may also be a relationship with an audience. Within each team there is a division of labour among the pre-designated positions which is set up by the legal requirements of the game rules, supplemented by team strategy. While actually in play, the flow of action indicated by the division of labour is further complicated by split-second judgements about capabilities, opportunities, tactics etc. Nevertheless, the preset division of labour remains a continued cooperative framework around which the game is organised from each side. In this situation, it is very often good, well-drilled team-work which secures victory, although clearly the mix of capabilities of the various players are also relevant. (It would be interesting to carry out a study of matches to endeavour to assess the degree of causal weight that could be assigned to good team-work as opposed to individual merit.)

As well as a smoothly-oiled cooperative structure, a team needs to hang together as a social unit to some degree. This could be described as team spirit or morale, and involves the social ties among the players and the overall social climate. The social structure will also reflect this social maintenance role: e.g. some players may be particularly good at encouraging others or smoothing over frictions. (Again, it would be interesting to study the causal impact of high morale. The nearest study we have to this may well be studies of small military units in wartime action. Certainly, such studies found that a major contribution to the fighting spirit of infantry lies in their immediate loyalties to their buddies: rather than any higher-level belief in the ultimate justice of their cause.) Morale and involvement in the group is sustained through symbols, rituals etc.

Contexts

So far, only internal aspects of structures have been considered. It is important that the relations between any social structure and its contextual and also subordinate social structures be explored. For a while, the study of social structures was locked into 'consensus' versus 'conflict' approaches, until it was sufficiently widely realised that it is artificial to see as polarities what are clearly merely the two ends of a continuum. It is a useful alliterative device to think of the general social condition in any social structure as being generally locatable on a 'scale' which ranges from collapse and chaos, through conflict, to competition, cooperation and then consensus and command. Each of these represents a zone on a continuum which describes how the average social unit in a social structure relates to others. Of course, in any structure the social conditions will differ from 'region' to 'region' and from time to time. This specification is useful only to alert analysts to the different social conditions which may pertain, and which they should bear in mind in conducting analyses, to remind them of the full extent of variation which is possible.

CONCLUSION

In sum, to develop appropriate theoretical approaches to the study of social structures, we must be alert to a considerable agenda of philosophical issues. To understand the vagaries and regularities of every day life, we need to work between the micro- and macro-levels, and between social and cultural modes of explanation. We need to be attuned to decision-making (and the efforts made in trying to realise those decisions) that individuals (and social groupings) make. In turn, we need to understand how people's (and groupings') opportunities for choice, and the choices they make, are shaped by the person's place in social structures, and the overall dynamics and long-term trajectory of that (or those) social structure(s). But to do all this, we need recourse to some more fine-grained tools of analysis. Chapter 5 will provide a range of these tools.

5

DIMENSIONS OF SOCIAL STRUCTURE
An analytical toolkit

A TOOL-RACK

Several quite different aspects of social structure have been focused on by different analysts (as indicated in Chapter 3). Sometimes, particular dimensions are thought to provide such a significant analytical purchase on understanding social structures that their proponents claim a privileged insight, and denigrate other approaches. However, in this chapter an eclectic viewpoint is adopted and each of ten different approaches to social structure is successively reviewed. My argument is that to successfully understand any social structure, many (maybe all) of these perspectives will need to be brought to bear. To some degree, the perspectives compete with each other, but they are not intrinsically incompatible. The tools covered are not exhaustive, but they do cover most of the tools needed to analyse social structures.

The perspectives are presented in an ordered sequence in which foundations are laid and then more particular aspects built on these. The sequence also moves from small-scale to larger-scale and from static to dynamic. However, to some extent this ordering is arbitrary and others might prefer different orders. The tools described in this chapter fit within the framework developed at the end of the previous chapter (Chapter 4), They spell out this framework and show how it can be put to work. Moreover, they draw on a wide range of the viewpoints discussed in the history chapter (Chapter 3) and some of the material in that chapter provides extra illustration of points made here.

The treatment given each conceptual tool is far from exhaustive. The central concept in each tool is briefly characterised and its historical background sketched. The emphasis is on the issues which arise in using each perspective as an analytical tool. In particular, I am concerned to bring to bear the contemporary 'state of knowledge' about each concept. Some guidance to further reading is provided through the references cited.

Levels of unit

The eleven conceptual tools fall into three main classes. The first group are perspectives which allow us to understand the 'architecture' of social structures

– how they are built. This sequence builds up from a foundation towards higher levels of organisation:

- Statuses and roles.
- Social networks and quasi-groups.
- Groups and organisations.
- Fields and institutional areas.

Perhaps the most difficult perspective to place in the order are 'social networks'. In a network approach, relations between nodes are studied, not characteristics of nodes themselves. Network linkages within any type of social entity (e.g. between individuals, but also between organisations) are possible. This interest in linkages can be taken to imply that network material should *follow* any approach looking at characteristics of social entities (on the grounds that you need to know something about x and about y before you examine their relationship). The problem then becomes that just as there are different levels of unit, so there can be relations between units at these different levels. For example, there can be relations between people, or between firms, or between countries, and one way of placing networks while retaining a hierarchy such as this would be to add networks in several times, after each level! Aggravating this, network analysts tend to see their perspective as crosscutting more orthodox sociological approaches and claim that the perspective can be applied irrespective of the level of the unit involved. However, it seems to me that the study of networks can be quite reasonably inserted between the study of people in roles and the study of collectivities.

Structural processes

The next five perspectives covered are orientated towards social processes. Having set up the structure, as it were, we can now set the structure to work, to mobilise it into operation. The social processes requiring separate treatment include:

- Social construction (setting up the boxes).
- Peopling (filling the boxes).
- Resourcing (producing from the boxes).
- Social change (changing the boxes).
- Life-courses (moving through the boxes).

Contexts

There are two final perspectives which do not quite so readily fit either of the above groups. There are two important contexts which bear on social structures. Social life takes place over time and is inevitably spatial, and these should be elements in analysis within each of the perspectives already covered.

However, since this contextual approach is sometimes forgotten, its importance is sign-posted by giving it separate attention.

ROLES/SOCIAL CATEGORIES

For many sociologists, the main building-block of social structure is the status-role. 'For most purposes the conceptual unit of the social system is the role' (Parsons and Shils 1951: 190). The usefulness of this concept is that it links both upwards to more comprehensive social structures (which can be seen as composed of combinations of status-roles) and also downwards to the nitty-gritty of the practice of everyday life (since people often relate their behaviour to the status-role position they hold).

Role analysis is built on the everyday point that we create our own identity and also relate with others in terms of key social characteristics, such as our (and their) age and gender, as well as many other societally-relevant and situationally-specific roles.

The concept is borrowed from the theatre where, of course, it refers to the characters in the cast which are played by actors. This metaphor is especially stressed by those focusing on the 'playing of roles': i.e. the performance of roles. What is more interesting, I think, is that other aspects of the theatrical metaphor are not stressed. The whole structural context that is indicated by looking beyond the playing of the actor's lines to consider the relevance of the playwright, the plot, and the relationships among the characters that the cast conjures up, is not attended to.

It seems very difficult to address status/role without quoting Shakespeare who shows a sequence of successive age-statuses. (Indeed, it seems part of the task of a role analyst to do so! Who am I to dodge this role-expectation?)

> All the world's a stage,
> And all the men and women merely players;
> They have their exits and their entrances;
> And one man in his time plays many parts,
> His acts being seven stages. At first the infant,
> mewling and puking in the nurses' arms.
> And then . . .
> (*As You Like It*: Act 2, Scene 7)

There is a central tension within the concept between the 'status-position' aspect of the concept, and the enactment 'role' aspect: between a position in a social structure and the behaviour and attitudes of a person occupying that social position. Clearly, these are interrelated aspects, and sometimes they are said to be 'two sides of the same coin'. However, the two aspects are differentially seized on by different approaches to the study of social roles: sometimes labelled the structural and the interactional views of roles.

There are many competing terminologies, so I will merely endeavour to be consistent and inform readers that if this terminology might not suit, to translate into their preferred terms. The central concept is that of status (or social position, although it can also be referred to in a generic sense as 'social role'). If a separate concept is needed to refer to the behavioural aspect of a status-position, 'role-performance' (or other appropriate term) should be used.

One difficulty with the term 'status' is that its normal English usage implies a definite hierarchical aspect. In this sociological usage, it does not have this meaning, and this can be confusing. Statuses, of course, can differ in their 'status', since hierarchical ranking is often an attribute of a status.

A status is a position in a framework of statuses to which are assigned behavioural standards, tasks and resources. The term has both denotations and connotations: statuses have both relatively up-front 'formal requirements' as well as a tail of less-defined 'informal requirements'. For example, teachers are not only expected to carry out the technical tasks of classroom teaching, but also may have further expectations placed on them of how they should conduct themselves in the community at large.

Any single status relates to several different audiences or complementary status-positions: e.g. school-teacher in relation to school-principal, fellow teachers, students, parents etc. Thus, it can be seen that the slice of the status relating to each separate one of these is a 'role-segment', and the related positions are 'role-complements'. The total set of audiences or role-complements can be referred to as the 'role-set', as Merton suggests in his conceptual elaboration:

> For some time now, at least since the influential writings of Ralph Linton on the subject, it has been recognised that two concepts – social status and social role – are fundamental to the description and the analysis of a social structure. By status Linton meant a position in a social system occupied by designated individuals: by role, the behavioural enacting of the patterned expectations attributed to that position. . . . Linton went on to observe that each person in society inevitably occupies multiple statuses, and for each of these statuses there is an associated role. . . . [But] we must note that a particular social status involves, not a single associated role, but an array of associated roles.
>
> (Merton 1968: 422)

Any person will occupy a range of status-positions at any one time, and even more over time. The set of statuses which a person occupies at one time can be referred to as their 'status-set': e.g. consisting of someone who is 'a teacher, wife, mother, Catholic, Republican and so on' (Merton 1968: 423). Certain combinations of these tend to be more complementary or more expected. Also, status-sets may be anchored in a crucial 'master-status' (e.g. ethnicity under many circumstances will be a crucial status; age or gender often can be too).

Finally, over time, people move in various ways through this social apparatus. Often there are quite regular sequences of roles or of statuses which people occupy one after another. These established sequences provide an over-time link between each component role or status in the sequence. Obvious examples include (especially for males) the sequence of apprenticeship, through journeyman status, to master artisan.

Uses of the concept

The first main use of status-role theory is as a framework on which to hang sociographic descriptions. Many studies have been carried out on particular statuses, as they are such convenient peg-boards. Such studies depict what tasks those in a status perform and other social characteristics which are assigned to them. Another usage is to develop a role-inventory, in which the array of statuses in a society is exhaustively listed – often what the tasks of each are. An example of this is Nadel's tabulation of some 35 male and 25 female roles in various Nuba tribes (1957: 62). Another common study is to catalogue which tasks are assigned to which statuses (e.g. men vs. women) across different societies. Indeed, this latter exercise of depicting a society's 'division of labour' has been referred to as a study of its 'social structure' (cf. Murdock 1949).

But these are just preliminaries for sociological explanations of people's behaviour in statuses. One line of explanation is cultural. Statuses are, to a considerable degree, a crystallisation of a bundle of norms or rules that are linked to a particular position. Indeed, one line of interpretation of roles is that each is neatly derived from the overall master-values of a particular culture and, as a result of being anchored in this more abstract cultural unity, the division into nicely-complementary roles ensures that society functions smoothly. However, social reality is seldom so neatly organised, to say the least.

Instead, it is more likely that these occupying roles are shaped by those in the surrounding role-structures. There are at least two main lines of explanation of people's behaviour and attitudes within status-and-role theory. One line of explanation involves people in statuses being 'socialised into' (i.e. learning) their roles, which they then 'internalise' (i.e. when the learning becomes part of their social identity). In this conception, the person learns the 'script' prepared by the social structure for that position, and usually does this so well that, after some fumbling starts, they are able to perform effortlessly on numerous occasions.

An alternative, and complementary, explanation emphasises 'social control' by those in the 'role-set'. The role-complements monitor the behaviour of the incumbent and endeavour to shape the incumbent's behaviour (and maybe their attitudes) to fit or suit the role-complement's views and expectations. This social control then locks the incumbents into patterns of reasonably acceptable actions.

Alongside social control is the aspect of social rewards. Role behaviour is as much shaped by reward-possibilities as it is by negative sanctions. In the

86

industrial relations arena much attention is given to the impact of different types of rewards for worker productivity and morale. For example, piece-rates can induce high output, but at a social cost. Associated with reward is the way of monitoring and measuring performance to allow the rewards to be assigned. This, too, can have a marked influence on what happens – among university academic staff, research tends to be rewarded, as research output appears to be more readily measured, whereas teaching performance is difficult to monitor and thus difficult to reward: therefore academics are more likely to put effort into their research at the expense of teaching or administration in order to obtain promotion.

The operation of reward and control mechanisms is seen as rather more complicated in the 'reference-group theory' approach (e.g. Merton 1968). This approach suggests that people more or less actively search out the reference framework they will relate to in occupying a status. Usually the role-complements, perhaps especially those in appropriate role-segments (e.g. a teacher or other professional colleagues), are the group to which someone orientates themselves. However, they may (also) fix their sights on quite a different reference-group. For example, upwardly mobile people may be more orientated to the views of the strata they are moving into than the strata from which they are coming. Some reference-groups may be abstract 'social categories' (sometimes technically referred to as 'non-membership groups': a rather indecorous term!) or even specific people who are chosen as 'role-models'.

An important point about status-positions is that it is through the ways in which they are organised that wider social structures can be held together or fissures created. Nadel (1957) had pointed out that very often different role-structures do not mesh with each other, so that wider social formations are not integrated through them – e.g. the age-order and gender-differentiation do not necessarily mesh. However, sometimes particular role-structures have a role in mediating between others (e.g. the judiciary and political leadership). One important way in which wider social orders are held together is through the mutual occupancy of statuses in status-sets. For example, it may be by virtue that, for a decision-maker who is both a business-person and a parent and partner, the business decision-making may at least be aware of the familial circumstances attending business change.

One implication of the multiple occupancy of statuses, and also of the multiple role-complements focusing on (parts of) particular statuses, is that quite a lot of conflict can be induced. In any particular status, and also for the set of statuses, an individual usually has only limited time (and other resources) which must be rationed around all their statuses or the role-segments. In addition, the different values associated with different statuses or role-segments can create strain. For example, principals, fellow-teachers, pupils and parents can all have rather different expectations of a teacher, and it can be very difficult to balance these into a coherent approach. Similarly, at the status-set level, a classic difficulty arises in endeavouring to balance family and work roles.

Merton has listed several mechanisms which provide status or role occupants with ways of handling these pressures. Tensions in role-sets may be handled by social mechanisms such as:

- differing intensity of role-involvement among those in the role-set (some role-relationships are central and others peripheral);
- differences in power among those involved in a role-set;
- insulating role-activities from observability by members of the role-set;
- observability by members of the role-set of their conflicting demands upon the occupants of a social status (this mechanism offsets 'pluralistic ignorance': the situation of unawareness of the extent to which values are in fact shared);
- social support by others in similar social statuses and thus with similar difficulties in coping with an unintegrated role-set;
- abridging the role-set (breaking off particular role-relationships).

(summarised in Crothers 1987: 96)

Similarly, Merton has suggested cognate mechanisms may handle stress in status-sets (Crothers 1987: 94). These include:

- perception by others in the status-set of competing obligations (e.g. employees are to a degree recognised to have families);
- shared agreement on the relative importance of conflicting status-obligations;
- self-selection of successive statuses that lessen differences between the values learned in earlier-held statuses and those pertaining in later statuses;
- self-selection of statuses which are 'neutral' to one another.

A major sociological theme has been that stress arises from awkward combinations of statuses that a person holds. Lenski (1954; see also Jackson and Curtis 1972) introduced the notion of 'status inconsistency' which hypothesised that those people occupying 'incongruent' status-sets might suffer increased social stress – or that there might be other consequences that flow from their 'cross-pressure' situation. There are a variety of effects which might follow from 'minority' or 'unusual' situations. This notion can be reasonably easily tested with survey data (technically, 'status inconsistencies' can turn up as 'interaction effects' where a category of one variable turns out to be linked to the category of another in its effects on attitudes or behaviour). Unfortunately, the body of evidence that has been assembled over the last few decades on this question has turned out to be ambiguous (there is a touch of irony in this). Some findings seem to have been a 'statistical artefact' of methods of research testing (Whitt 1983) and some social researchers have concluded that the general thrust of the evidence is negative. A difficulty is that such interactions tend not to be very stable across different research populations, and often, even if they are found, their effect is trivial.

Rose Coser (1991) has moved beyond this stress or conflict view to emphasise the positive opportunities opened up by more complex status-sets. She argues that it is within the very interstices opened-up by complex status-sets that wider degrees of individual freedom can come to be realised. One aspect of this is that people learn more sophisticated social skills – including linguistic flexibility – as they learn to handle role complexity. It may also be that more energy is generated as a result of the interplay between statuses. There are also possibilities for integration and for innovation.

History

There is a long trail of precursors who used a status-role concept: all the founding fathers, for a start. However, the concept was firmly put on the social science agenda in the 1930s by Mead, Moreno and Linton. These three were the founders of rather different traditions of role analysis.

- *Linton* (an anthropologist) saw role as a segment of a culture and stressed the functional importance of people being assigned roles for the smooth running of a society.
- *Mead* developed what became the strong current of 'symbolic interaction-ism' which stressed the importance, in any ongoing social interaction, of the interplay between the expectations of the various parties: a process termed 'role-taking'.
- *Moreno's* conception of 'role-playing' was seen as having educational and therapeutic values since a person was required to adopt the different viewpoints held by people with different roles, which would give them an insight into how a person in that position might relate to the world.

It is particularly important to keep the two main threads of development separate: too often discussions of role lapse into an interactional viewpoint of role-taking or perhaps role-playing instead of retaining the structural conception of Linton.

The 1950s and 1960s were the 'golden age' for the development of various aspects of role theory, and during this period there was an enormous expansion of concepts and terms. More recently, interest has faltered and the concept has come under considerable criticism (see Biddle 1987; Handel 1979). Never-theless, many theorists still refer to the concept (e.g. Bauman 1990) and even the critics re-establish the term in practice (e.g. Giddens 1984).

Criticisms

The concept has been heavily criticised from several directions (e.g. Giddens 1979: 116–17; Connell 1979 [1983]):

- Since role-language is commonly used by people themselves, for sociologists to merely adopt the argot of actors may be fruitful for enhancing description, but hardly adds an explanation.
- It too readily assumes that role requirements are given and must be met.
- It 'presume(s) both a unity of normative expectations that cohere to form the role, and a consensus in a social system about what these expectations are' (Comell 1979: 204).
- It 'is a major prop to the Parsonian view of the overriding importance of values or norms in social analysis'.
- It is prone to allowing almost everything to become swallowed up in role analysis.
- It is difficult to ascertain to what level of detail action is controlled by a role (e.g. are its more technical aspects also to be seen as controlled socially?).
- Role-frames cannot be aggregated to form a coherent whole for the whole of a society.
- Ultimately, role analysis is psychological, since the social controllers need to be motivated to sanction role-occupants.
- 'It is the practical ideology embedded in the daily work of counsellors, social workers, teachers and personnel officers so far as they are concerned with shaping people and their activity to the requirements of the system, i.e. forestalling resistance' (Connell 1979: 204).

Finally, there is an array of ethno-methodological and related critiques of the role concept. Such criticisms deconstruct the role concept and indicate that it should be seen as a 'constructed account' put forward by the actor. For example, Hilbert argues from an ethno-methodological perspective that 'actors do produce [stable role behaviour] not only when called upon, but whenever, for one reason or another, they need to provide for the typicality, the reasonableness, the competence of their socially accountable behaviour' (Hilbert 1981: 220). However, this view seems to overlook the point that such 'accounts' are surely also pre-given 'scripts' in very many situations.

Needed revamping and extension

There is little doubt that role analysis seems too readily to fall into theoretical sloppiness. Much tighter use of the concept is required to overcome some of its limitations. In addition, there are several lines of extension that are needed to fructify role analysis.

A major limitation in the development of role theories has been in not exploring the structuring aspect implicit in the theatrical metaphor. In plays, the playwright (not to mention the director) is clearly important in structuring not just the 'parts', but the relationships among them. But this aspect is seldom explored in role studies: the 'social rule theorists' are the main exception (see Burns and Flam 1987). Yet, some role-structures are very much designed and operated by controllers (e.g. managers of capitalist firms) and many other role-structures are held in order by common, planned frameworks. So, role studies should focus more on the 'playwrights' and 'directors': which is related to the concept of 'moral entrepreneur'. Many role-structures are constituted with an asymmetrical imbalance between the ruler-setters and the rule-followers.

Also, roles need to be more firmly linked to the allocation and distribution of resources and to material and symbolic production, rather than emphasising the more normative aspects of the concept. Most roles are involved in the production of something or other, and the allocation of resources to a role-structure, and the distribution of resources within it, are central to its operation. While this is often stressed in descriptive accounts by sociographers, it is seldom theorised.

An ideological difficulty is that an uncritical adoption of role terms can unwittingly lead a social analyst into becoming a social control agent. For a start, sociologists' accounts of roles (e.g. what tasks are assigned them) may act to freeze or idealise what is a rather more subtle and fluid reality. Then, once these ideals are established, social counsellors may try to shape recalcitrant people into the roles that they have established. Instead, role analysis might be used to reconstruct role-structures along quite different lines than those pertaining in present arrangements. One example of the involvement of role analysis with a social movement concerned with change is the use of 'sex role theory' by feminists. 'First wave feminism' was alert to the social (as opposed to biological) shaping of sex roles, and the long, steadily-deepening socialisation which lead into the adult models of 'men' and 'women'. Legitimised by feminist social ideology, the obvious change strategies were to attempt to emphasise the arbitrariness of expectations in relation to sex roles and to 'clean up' the socialisation process, so that it was less gender-biased. Prime targets were those (males) who made up and applied the rules on which (personal) characteristics were deemed appropriate for particular roles. Decisive and early gains could be readily made using these tactics, and they also could be assisted by social research (e.g. content analyses of primer readers which showed the extent to which women were seldom depicted in occupational roles, especially higher-status occupational roles). However, the gains made by this approach gradually wore down, since the room to manoeuvre in changing roles is limited without implementing deeper changes in the social structure.

Summary

Despite the fusillade of criticism, the concept of status-role remains a standard concept in the repertoire of many social analysts. Many who disclaim its use or ignore roles theoretically nevertheless smuggle it into their work, even when they do not seem to realise that they are implicitly doing so. Some conception of status-role is an essential building block for social analysis: it is an essential element in the social analyst's toolkit. But, in itself, the role framework merely maps the social phenomena to be explained. There is a considerable range of different theories that can be used within this framework, and care should be taken that appropriate ones are used. In particular, quite different mechanisms about how roles are linked to resulting actions can be invoked.

NETWORKS AND 'QUASI-GROUPS'

Network analysis draws out the everyday point that one way of locating yourself in relation to other people is not just in terms of what characteristics you have (e.g. gender, age), but 'who you know', or more generally what sort of people you associate with.

Although others have used this term in different ways, notably Dahrendorf (1968) and Mayer (1966), I portray networks as 'quasi-groups' – i.e. as a form of social organisation that links people, but which need not be as formally organised and clearly bounded as 'proper' groups are.

The root metaphor in this approach is that of webs and graphs. Fischer puts it well:

> Society affects us largely through tugs on the strands of our networks – shaping our attitudes, providing opportunities, making demands on us, and so forth. And it is by tugging at those same strands that we make our individual impact on society – influencing other people's opinions, obtaining favours from 'insiders', forming action groups.
>
> (cited in Wilson 1983: 54)

Over at least the last three decades, a network approach to studying social structure has been champing at the bit, trying to breakthrough into the mainstream of sociological consciousness with its message. Great promise is held out for a revolutionary break-through.

The possibilities for reducing some of the messiness of social life to sparse, clean, graphic, mathematical models are particularly appealing to some in the network approach. However, although some network analysis material is published in mainstream journals and by mainstream book publishers, the mainstream of sociologists have yet to heed the call. It still seems that network analysis remains 'ghettoised' on the margins of sociology. Indeed, network specialists have withdrawn themselves and much network material is published in a couple of specialist journals. Yet this approach is indispensable (some would say central) to understanding social structures.

Network analysis focuses on the links between social entities and not the characteristics of those entities. Analyses examine the more basic relationship structure underlying the myriad links which are the surface manifestations of networks, and then explore how a social unit's position within a network shapes its actions. Another, more aggregated, way of conceptualising network linkages is in terms of Bourdieu's concept of 'social capital', which has also been picked up by network analysts such as Coleman (1990) and Burt (1992). Social capital is seen by Bourdieu as, in effect, the 'linkage reach' of people and especially the extent to which they can convert other forms of capital into effective use.

One strength of network approaches is that they detect patterns of social life operating beneath and around more formal structures. For example, working class residential communities may not be studded with links through formal organisations and, therefore, may appear to the casual observer to be devoid of social structure. In fact, they may be quite tightly interlaced by informal social links. Another strength is that network analysis can probe behind surface patterns of links to show indirect paths of contact, mediated through other people or collective units. Yet another emphasis in network analysis is on concrete links between actual units, rather than more vague pictures of expectations and possibilities, which is where role analysis often leaves matters.

Almost any form of social entity can be the anchoring-points for examining the networks which link them: e.g. individuals, organisations, communities as well as nations. Indeed, one of the big appeals of network analysis is the very range of social groupings that have been covered: e.g. the collection edited by Wellman and Berkowitz (1988) covers kinship ties, community involvements, informal work cliques, patron-client relations, markets, international trade patterns, citation links, and job vacancy allocations. This breadth in subject-matter allows a far-flung alliance of analysts from quite different subject-matter specialties to be built around a common analytical framework and research methodology.

Network analysts vary in the vigour and exclusiveness of their stance: the most radical denigrate any attention to people's opinions and views, seeing these as emanations of their network position. The *form* of relationships is often stressed over their *content*. Such an abstract approach aids communication between sociologists across wide-flung topic-areas. Many see the metaphor that underlies their approach as being so powerful that only a network approach is able to reveal the operations of social structure. For some, any other approach to social analysis is invalid. Their argument is quite simple: if social structure by definition concerns relationships among people and other social entities, these relationships should be studied directly. The work of other approaches is seen as essentially social psychological or as 'essentialist', dealing with units or with aggregates of units, not the structures which are built between these.

Strong claims of explanatory power are often made . For example, Burt argues that his particular 'Structural Holes' approach, which focuses on unfilled gaps in network structures, delivers a punch which other approaches slide away from. (Similar claims have been made in most other accounts of network analysis.)

The structural hole argument escapes the debilitating social science practice of using player attributes for explanation. The relations that

93

intersect to create structural holes give a player entrepreneurial opportunities to get higher rates of return. The player in whom the relations intersect – black, white, female, male, old, young, rich, poor – is irrelevant to the explanation. Competition is not about being a player with certain physical attributes; it is about securing productive relationships. Physical attributes are a correlate, not a cause, of competitive success. Holes can have different effects for people with different attributes or for organisations of different kinds, but these differences in effect occur because the attributes and organisational forms are correlated with different positions in social structure. The manner in which a structural hole is an entrepreneurial opportunity for informational benefits and control benefits is the bedrock explanation that carries across player attributes, populations and time. The task for the analyst is to cut past the spurious correlation between attributes and outcomes to reach the underlying social structural features that cause the outcome.

(Burt 1992: 4)

History

The network metaphor stretches back at least to Simmel (Scott 1991; which, incidentally, is the best historical source). Informal and underdeveloped network studies were carried out in the 1930s in industrial sociology. Cliques were outlined in the Hawthorne and other 'plant sociology' studies of this period, and their operation in affecting productivity discussed. At this time, too, Moreno developed sociograms to describe network relations. While around mid-century both Radcliffe-Brown and Nadel briefly mentioned a web metaphor and have, as a result, been acclaimed by network analysis historians – this influence is very weak. Rather, it was in the mid-1950s with Bott's studies of East London families and Barnes' study of Norwegian fishing villages that the empirical study of networks was put on a firm footing. Barnes was interested in the way in which particular fishing crews were mobilised from among the range of possible recruits within a village. Bott (1957) found that working class families tended to have strong matrilocally biased linkages between daughter and mother, and that this pattern affected the family division of labour and visiting patterns, among other effects.

From then on, network studies gradually spread within anthropology, sociology and political science. Earlier studies tended to have firm ethnographic foundations and to provide richly nuanced understandings of networks. However, there has also been a more formal, mathematical approach to networks. This approach has been particularly fostered as network analysts have tapped into reams of already-quantified information about relationship linkages. Some of this type of data has included information on interlocking directorships (those company directors who are on the boards of several companies) or various links between countries (such as trade, aid or similarity in voting patterns in the UN). Often, this data was digital (link/non-link) or quantitative and was readily available. The use of such data-sets, more formalisation of mathematically-based models, and the availability of computer programmes to analyse them has propelled the network analysis paradigm forward, but it has tended to curtail a more qualitative interest in studying networks ethnographically (as the earlier studies had done).

By the mid-1970s, the field developed enough critical mass and density of interconnection to become institutionalised – with its own official association or network, conference circuit and journals. (Ironically, this process is quite self-exemplifying!) The field continues to develop but, unfortunately, has not widened its circle of *afficionados*: perhaps the networking of network analysts is poor!

Theoretical models

A very important distinction is that between 'network cohesion' and 'structural equivalence' (Burt 1987). The two ideas posit quite different ways of examining nodes and their linkages. The network cohesion concept links those who interact with each other. For example, in a medical centre, each set of patients, receptionists, practice nurses and doctors form a network based around each particular doctor. However, each of these four types of position is the basis for network links based on the 'structural equivalence' of the people concerned. That is, each plays an equivalent role in 'their' network and analysis can be built around this similarity. Often these positions are, in fact, also socially prescribed status-roles, but they need not be. Nodes can occupy 'structurally equivalent' positions without this being formally recognised by the culture. Indeed, as Scott (1991: 127) suggests, it may very well be that new roles emerge in this way, out of interactional patterns. This latter situation is particularly interesting as it is a contribution that network analysis is particularly suitable to picking up.

While it is interesting that network analysts have come up with several major concepts for describing network patterns, it is necessary to probe for the explanatory ideas underlying these models of networks in order for network analysis to provide a theoretical contribution to sociology. Unfortunately, this theoretical contribution is not as readily apparent as the volume-level of network propaganda might suggest! Indeed, at several points over the last few decades network theorists have themselves lamented the 'theory-research' gap (e.g. Granovetter 1979). On the other hand, Emirbayer and Goodwin (1994) provide a theoretical critique of different emphases with the overall network approach. Certainly, this area of study has been driven far more by methodological concerns than by theoretical ideas. While this is excusable given the complexity and awkwardness of the data, it is not good enough in the longer run.

This is not to say that this area is void of theoretical ideas. Indeed, there are many very important concepts which have been developed. One key idea is the importance of 'weak ties'. As opposed to the 'strong ties' which bind groups together, the much more extended range of 'friends of friends' may be particularly important on some matters. (Network analysis incorporates nodes connected by strong ties, too, but is particularly effective in picking up the looser and lighter web of more extended linkages.) In several studies of how people obtain services (e.g. an abortionist, a job) it has been found that weak ties have been more effective than strong ties. This is because only a limited stock of information circulates within a closed group, whereas the surveillance range of a whole number of weak ties is far wider. Thus, more widely-flung contacts are likely to hold a much greater stock of information, even if this web of weak ties is not very systematic or efficient in passing that information on.

Another key idea is that of 'connectivity'. Formally separated social units may be coordinated or controlled behind the scenes by a web of inter-connections. Indeed, analysts of the economic power élite which is con-sidered to run the business world have developed a variety of models of how interconnectedness is achieved behind the backs of markets which are apparently populated by a host of independent businesses. It has been shown that there are:

- controlling effects of an upper class operating through policy think-tanks and foundations;
- controlling effects of major property-owning families through family trusts;
- controlling effects through major banks which can be at the centre of groupings of companies; and
- controlling effects through business empires built up by acquisition as much as merger.

Such links can be measured and their patterns modelled.

Another important idea is that of 'structural balance'. From examining triads of relations among three people (or nodes), it can be readily seen that some triads are balanced whereas others are unbalanced. For example, if A is dominant over B and B dominant over C, the triad is balanced if then A is dominant over C. Indeed, one might expect this to occur naturally anyway, although empirically there are exceptions which are unbalanced. This type of analysis is interesting in providing predictions about the longer-term stability of groups, based on the characteristics of their constituent triads.

A recently developed key idea concerns 'structural holes' (Burt 1992). These are the gaps in a network pattern, and they provide entrepreneurial opportunities for those in the existing pattern to move in to exploit. This is part of a sociological contribution to understanding the links between firms in markets, although such structural holes can occur in a wide variety of social structures.

Applications

Network concepts have been used across a wide variety of settings. One important area of application has been in the area of social stress and disease, where many studies of 'social support' or caring networks have been carried out (Veiel and Baumann 1992). A key idea, here, has been that people who are socially isolated are more vulnerable and less able to call on resources to overcome difficulties which they may have. It is not surprising that network ideas fit nicely into this concern.

Network analysis might be described as a shared methodology (although there are varieties within this) around which are draped several useful ideas and the whole imbued with much missionary enthusiasm. This approach is so important that it should be better related to mainstream sociology.

GROUPS/ORGANISATIONS

In early US sociology, the subject of sociology was sometimes taken to be the relations between groups and among organisations. Certainly, sociologists should be alert to the existence of formal groups and organisations. Indeed, it is a topic that has received too little attention, and collectivities are too seldom built into widely-circulating sociological theories. This, of course, is highly ironic since this is surely a core area of sociology. On the other hand, the very active area of the sociology of organisations is a somewhat sequestered area of study, which has had little impact on more general social theory. It has been developing links with business studies instead. The study of those collectivities (e.g. primary groups) other than formal organisations is rather less developed.

This sociological slighting of collective entities is surely at strong variance with their dominance in social experience.

> Our society is an organisational society. We are born in organisations, educated by organisations, and most of us spend much of our lives working for organisations. We spend much of our leisure time paying, playing and praying in organisations. Most of us will die in an organisation, and when the time comes for burial, the largest organisation of them all – the State – must grant official permission.
>
> (Etzioni 1964: ix)

Moreover it is reasonably easy to develop evidence to show how rapidly organisations have grown in number and size over the last century in terms of:

- growth in number of profit-making corporations;
- proportions of people and of collective entities involved in legal actions;
- attention to people and collective entities in newspaper coverage.

(Coleman 1982: 10–12; see also Cohen et al. 1990 and Warner et al. 1967)

Despite the immense breadth of different types of organisation and their penetration into everyday lives, their study has been generally assigned to the sociology of organisations. Only a few types of organisations tend to be excepted from the far-flung interest-span of the sociology of organisations: perhaps the study of collective behaviour and smaller structures such as families and households, together with larger ones such as the State or national societies. The more formal sociology of organisations is supplemented by a coterie of organisational studies within particular institutional areas and carried out by social scientists attached to other disciplines or study-areas – e.g. political scientists study political parties; educationists study schools; management studies people businesses. But I do not wish to merely report a summary of organisational studies in this section, as many treatments are available (e.g. see Ahrne 1994). I will draw on this literature, but my main concern is to demonstrate the continuity of the study of organisations within the overall analysis of social structures, and this requires recourse to broader literatures.

A major push for the recognition of collectivities has come from James Coleman. Coleman has argued across several decades (1982; 1990; see Hindess 1989 for a critique) that there are two types of 'persons': natural and corporate. Coleman then cross-tabulates the possible linkages between the two kinds of person: natural persons can relate to other natural persons and collective persons to other collective persons and, of course, natural and collective persons can interrelate (see Table 5.1). It is the last two types of relationships which then become of particular interest.

Table 5.1 Person/corporate relations

Subject	Object	
	Person	Corporate Actor
Person	1	2a
Corporate Actor	2b	3

Source: from Coleman 1982: 20

Corporate entities are further classified into primordial (e.g. the family) and constructed (e.g. corporations). Where primordial entities are composed of fixed positions occupied by unique persons (who are not interchangeable), the modern forms are a structure of positions which can be changed and in which the occupants can be changed. The key change is that the modern organisation is a legal entity, which can act on its own, distinct from its members. This social invention allows for innovations to be much more readily adopted.

But this flexibility is a two-edged sword. On the one hand, the often oppressive primordial structures are broken up and people are allowed more freedom, since they are now socially controlled only in respect of each of their various roles rather than their fixed family-kinship position. On the other hand, since so many natural persons are employed by collective organisations, their purposes in life are bent to the wishes of these structures. The intense web of face-to-face social linkages that formerly pertained is now reduced and subject to severe intrusion from collective persons: e.g. schools and advertisers. The relation between collective entities and natural persons is asymmetrical. Organisations are obtrusive and intrusive and difficult to gain information about or to control. Perhaps the final irony is that, to obtain some leverage over corporations, natural people may resort to agencies such as the state or to trade unions: but these too can be very distant from and unresponsive to citizens' or members' wishes.

Making people into groups

There has been much discussion across many areas of sociology, about how people loosely aggregated within social categories may become more tightly welded into collectivities or organisations. The classic discussion was that of Marx concerning the revolutionary consciousness of the working class. To enable collective revolutionary action, the working class requires:

- to widely share immiseration;
- to have punctured the dominant ideology which cloaks the reality of their situation;
- to have begun to replace this with a working class ideology; and
- to build up some organisational capacity (e.g. through trade unions).

Merton's views are more general (Crothers 1987: 97; Merton 1968). He distinguishes between categories, collectivities and groups. Members of categories share statuses and thereby similar interests and values, although not necessarily through shared interaction or a common and distinctive body of norms. Collectivities share norms and have a sense of solidarity, while members of groups interact with each other and share a common identity, which is also attributed to them by others. But he does not then go on to provide a sociological explanation of how groupings might move up (or for that matter down) this hierarchy of levels.

Other sociologists have sketched similar scenarios of group-formation (more is discussed on this in the 'Social construction' section later in this chapter). However, in general, it should be said that this topic of structure-building is an area of considerable theoretical importance that has not been adequately studied.

Most studies of organisations assume the organisation's existence, and have gone on to study their characteristics. The study of organisations can be seen (as indeed Coleman has argued) to some degree as the study of individuals raised to a higher power. Many of the same points are common to the sociological study of both. Each organisation is in some part unique, but also shares similarities in its attributes with other organisations. They interact with other organisations and can bunch together to form further, higher-level (meta-) organisations. They persist, they change, they are born, they die. However, the metaphor does not carry over exactly as, unlike people, organisations can have major bits broken off, or added to, and can interact with people as well as other collectivities. A further and central discontinuity with this individualistic analogy is that organisations tend to be multi-layered. Any organisation can be a veritable 'Russian doll' of nested sub-organisations, and there can also be layers of people who are affected beyond the usual organisational boundaries. Social patterns can also crosscut the layers and boundaries of organisations.

Attributes of organisations often are similar to those of individuals. Organisations can have ages, histories, sizes etc. They can have 'personalities': a 'corporate culture'. Certainly organisations *do* things and can have a set of attitudes (policy). Studies of groupings of organisations can be carried out (much as studies of groupings of individuals) and the patterning of their various attributes related to each other. It is possible to get an understanding of why organisations act in similar ways by endeavouring to relate their actions to attributes they may have in common. Network studies among, as well as within, organisations can also be carried out. In sum:

> In analysing an organisation, the major independent variables are the formal institutions in terms of which social conduct is organised: the division of labour, the hierarchy of offices, control and sanctioning mechanisms, production methods, official rules and regulations, per- sonnel practices and so on. The major dependent variables are the results accomplished by operations and the attachment of its members to the organisation, as indicated by productive efficiency, changes effected in the community (say, a decline in crime rates), turnover, satisfaction with work, and various other effect criteria. To explain the relationship between these two sets of abstract variables, it is necessary to investigate the processes of social interaction and the interpersonal relations and group structures.
>
> (Blau cited in Calhoun *et al*. 1990: 17)

Sociologists of organisations have also developed a distinct vocabulary which identifies several further major features of organisations. They are seen as having goals, an internal structure, technology and resources, and a surround- ing environment. In pursuit of their goals, they deploy their material and human resources to suit the key features of their technology and organisational framework in order to produce whatever goods and services is their purpose.

Many organisational analysts cleave to a view of organisations as being organised more-or-less rationally: that their goals provide clear guidance, decisions are rationally made within the parameters set by the goals, and the organisation is rationally organised in terms of its means for reaching these goals. This concern of organisations with rationality contrasts strongly with the considerable inefficiency of most other types of social entity. It provides a basis for expecting clearer patterns of similarity among organisations. Cleaner scientific results in studying organisations might be expected, since organisations facing similar situations are likely to come up with similar solutions and therefore be similarly organised. However, the actual practice of the study of organisations has been to progressively withdraw from this assumption of rationality. Rather, organisations are increasingly represented as being messy, chaotic, and operating complexly in relation to the multiple contingencies they face. If formal organisations are like this, other social entities are likely to be even more sloppy in their structuring and therefore require that much more complexity to be recognised in their study.

It has been found that organisations, far from being quite static in their pattern, have changed their practices of management over time. As a result, much of the recent effort in organisational studies has gone into the tracking of changes in organisational form. The contemporary literature is often exciting in its depictions of new forms of organisation. One lesson that has been increasingly drawn is that it is not enough to concentrate on the internal operation of organisations, but that they must be understood within the framework of the wider social order.

History

The way in which organisational 'rationality' has been seen has differed markedly over time. These differences can be illustrated by examining the history of the sociology of organisations. This stretches back at least to World War I, when Max Weber's experience as a temporary administrator of military hospitals led him to formulate an 'ideal type' of a bureaucracy. (The characteristics that Weber identified in these efficient human administrative machines have already been noted in Chapter 3.)

However, Weber did not focus only on the internal arrangements of formal organisations. Rather, these are located as but one type of 'administration' among several. There are particular societal conditions when bureaucracies, rather than other forms of administration, are likely to prevail. So Weber provides a sociology of organisations. He also provides a social critique. Bureaucracies can be seen as a component in a grim dark soulless process of the increasing rationalisation of human life. For example, whatever hopes a socialist revolution might have, it was sure in the longer term to be ground under the heel of the faceless human machines which would be set up to implement the revolution's goals.

Since World War II, organisational studies have blossomed. Not surprisingly, their analysis has spread across several areas of study including management studies. Most studies have bounced off various aspects of Weber's model, although this classic formulation has only survived as a statement of an extreme type which few actual organisations approximate. Formal organisations were soon revealed to work as much through informal channels of communication and influence as through the official structure of their 'line of command'. Attempts were made to explore relationships between various attributes of organisations (e.g. size, technology etc.) and how these might relate to various aspects of the environments organisations operated within.

Meyer (in Calhoun *et al.* 1990) has summarised well some key aspects of the changing perspectives on organisations. He suggests that Weber's views on organisations have usually, in effect, been 'boiled down' to a simplified 'structure-efficiency' model because of 'its simplicity, consistency with classical administrative thinking, and apparent testability' (1990: 193). This model posits – quite contrary to the ordinary citizen's views on 'red tape'! – that, since bureaucracy is a rational way of organising, efficiency will result.

The early round of post-World War II case studies of organisations supplemented Weber's model by showing that, in reality, the operations of bureaucracies lead to 'dysfunctions' (e.g. that welfare bureaucracies stigmatise their clientele). Meyer suggests that early 1960s quantitative studies of organisations which spent much time in measuring organisational structures revealed size effects that were directly or indirectly linked to efficiency, but did not strongly support this model. Moreover, these studies tended to ignore the environment of organisations in their more immediate quest to establish an understanding of the internal arrangements of organisations.

He then summarises in a few swift bold strokes the next twenty years of organisational research from the late 1960s onwards as involving three steps, with each emphasising environmental factors.

First, the structure-efficiency model was extended to accommodate environmental variation. Second, survival outcomes were substituted for efficiency outcomes. Third, efficiency was removed altogether from the model so that the central premise of organisational sociology became the environmental determination of organisational structures.

(Meyer 1990: 199)

In the first of these phases, the 'contingency' and 'resource dependence' approaches to organisations both argued that rather different forms of organisation were appropriate to different environmental and technology situations. In the following phase, one major approach has been the 'population ecology' approach in which the focus was on the processes through which particular types of organisation were developed and whether or not members of particular types of organisations survived. This approach was valuable in pointing out that the current stock of organisations is, in fact, a subset of the longer-term flow of organisational start-ups and failures.

In the current phase of organisational study, Meyer argues that the rationality and efficiency considerations imposed from the controlling levels beyond organisations are now seen as most critical. He argues that particular organisational forms are now chosen or designed to suit the requirements of these controlling authorities. Meyer refers to these as 'commodity organisations' since, in this regime, they are definitely creatures of the powers that be.

More recent approaches to organisations tend to emphasise their institutional or cultural uniquenesses (see Reed and Hughes 1992; Scott 1993). The role of shared meaning is considered central and the organisations are seen as far more fragile and ephemeral than in earlier viewpoints. This parallels similar shifts in viewpoint across other areas of social structural study.

To conclude, some general lessons can be drawn. The analysis of organisations requires extra skills of its own, although it also shares much in common with other sociological approaches. The sociological analysis of organisations must only not remain confined to individual organisations, or to patterns of organisations, or even the interaction between organisations and their environments, but also needs to cover the effect on social life of the whole layer of organisations which so dominate modern societies.

INSTITUTIONAL AREAS/FIELDS

An important sociological conception is the image that societies are composed of assemblages of institutions, often arrayed within particular institutional areas (e.g. family, economy, religion etc.). In this vision, it is readily seen that the 'content' of each social area differs from that of others, and that this content is particularly relevant to its analysis. Particular central values and norms are seen as flavouring the working of each institutional area. It may also be that particular institutional areas are characterised by particular structural configurations: their environment gives the social forms in a particular area some unique features.

This area of investigation is usually not adequately covered in sociology. How institutional areas work is seldom made problematic. This is because institutional areas are so often the unexamined context of sociological specialities, or form the focus for a separate discipline or interdisciplinary field. Once the 'long march through the institutional areas' (family, economy, religion etc.) has been completed within an introductory sociological course, concern with institutional areas in their own right often fades from sociological attention.

In older sociologies, sometimes a 'billiard-ball' model of societies was used: societies were seen as a set of institutions – the economy, polity, religion etc. – and the relations between each were plotted (e.g. Weber is depicted as exploring the relations between religion and the economy in particular societies). But today, few studies focus particularly on institutional areas as a unit of analysis.

One very interesting, but unfortunately fugitive, study is Storer's (1966) analysis (adapted from Parsons) of the key features of science, the family, politics and religion: each is seen as being built around a unique product or type of reward (i.e. creativity, sex, power, the sacred) and each is portrayed as jealously guarding its own boundaries from the others.

Bourdieu's image of a field is useful to map an institutional area (see the discussion in Chapter 3). He sees the economy, polity etc. in modern societies as fields with their own internal logic of development and relative autonomy, although he is also concerned with their interrelations. Each field has its own values and goals, and there is struggle among those in the field (employing whatever capitals they have command over and which have legitimacy in that field) for the right to set the standards, and to exercise power, in that field. In addition, Bourdieu sees linkages between institutional fields, and that fields have their own tendency to reflect wider society and also to shuck off any (too close) overlaps from other institutional areas. His approach also allows investigation of the extent to which, in any social formation, there have developed separate fields: it is not assumed that there is any particular menu of institutional areas. However, the mix of available types of capital in a society may structure the range of fields which have a separate existence.

It might be added that fields also differ in terms of their organisational arrangements: whereas the formal economy is organised into firms, together with central coordinating institutions such as the stock market, the family/ household sector of society merely consists of endless numbers of small units with only the most occasional formal organisation claiming to represent the interests of some particular fraction of households.

Other conceptions which are used to understand environing 'fields' include studies of inter-organisational relations and markets. Inter-organisational relations has become a subject-area in its own right (for literature reviews, see Ahrne 1994; Aldrich and Marsden 1988; Nohria and Eccles 1992).

Such inter-organisational studies often take a network perspective, although some are conducted under a 'political economy' rubric. Many of these studies show how alliances of organisations can be mobilised to work together to shape broad areas of policy development or market operation. For example, the oil industry in the USA organised to squash possible governmental flight regulations that would have then exposed commercially secret data on the paths of exploration flights. Another example concerns agricultural workers, stuck with low wage rates, who were able to mobilise their affiliates to put pressure on the networks of the employing super-company, which then eventually raised the wages. Much activity in social formations involves complex, shifting and often fragile relations among blocs of organisations.

Another key metaphor is that of the market. A market is a particular type of inter-organisational framework which provides a mechanism through which the operations of the various units can be coordinated. This ideal-type model can also be held up against at least partially similar structural alternatives to examine differences in their mode of operation: e.g. command economies. A classic market is supposedly one where there is a range of different units of somewhat similar size, where each has little effect on other units and where there is a good flow of information. Unfortunately, these particular character- istics of such seldomly found-in-reality ideal markets are infrequently spelled out, yet this is the type of environing structure which is assumed by many micro-level social theorists: e.g. those using a rational choice model.

Not only do the assumptions about the types of market structure which pertain have to be spelled out, but something of the sociological complexities of market structures need to be explored. Economists and market analysts are aware of a range of market imperfections, but they do not always press on to explore the range of units operating in markets (e.g. in terms of their range of size, resources etc.). As sociologists have pointed out, although this is usually ignored by economists (other than 'institutional economists'), market-structures do not arise spontaneously but are socially constructed.

The social construction of markets involves several meanings. They have their own special organisations to enable the coordination to be achieved, and are governed by institutionalised rules which guide conduct within them. They rest, too, on common understandings. 'Trust', for example, must be ensured for markets to operate readily. Otherwise partners to a transaction cannot be assured of adequate performance. Moreover, there is nothing magical about the institutional arrangements of any market: despite quite hegemonic new right ideological views on this matter! Market-structures themselves can be constituted or reconstituted to suit (governmental or other) policy objectives.

Another unnecessary simplification which traps some analysts is the idea that there is a single overall market. Rather, there is often a whole array of different markets which are only loosely and complexly interrelated. For example, there can be labour markets, commodity markets, financial markets and so on. Each of these operates with different units and somewhat different commodities, and the whole cannot be entirely boiled down into a single overall homogeneous structure.

Finally, it is useful to remember the range of relations which may pertain in any market. Besides competition among units (which is the prescribed form of relationship), there are other possibilities including oligopoly and monopoly, in which competition is constrained in the interests of dominant parties. Where a market is not operating within well-established confines, it is possible for competition to be eclipsed by conflict or to degenerate into chaos.

Although the internal organisation of an institutional area may take the structure of being a market, this form is *particularly* appropriate only to the description of economies. Other institutional areas tend to have rather different internal arrangements. Their form and content tend to intertwine in the following discussion, although ultimately these should be kept separate.

An institutional environment which differs from economic markets is that centred on the government. This sector involves the ordinary public as 'citizens' rather than 'customers' and marches to the beat of rather different requirements. Of recent years, however, new right ideologists have increasingly attempted to subvert these differences and to remake the state sector along the lines of straight capitalism. As well as being an important area of society, a state

105

can be a significant set of organisations leading many other areas of social activity. One important role the State often plays is in rule-setting and enforcement of these rules in the markets which the various other social units are, in turn, embedded within.

Beyond the economy and polity lie other sectors. A third sector is the voluntary and non-profit one, which operates according to yet a further set of rules, but which is also under siege from both governmental and, especially, capitalist modes of operation. The current 'mixed' operation of some voluntary sub-sectors has been described as a 'quasi-market'. Another institutional area is focused on the family and household operation within communities. There are a wide variety of other institutional areas which might also deserve separate attention.

A useful distinction to invoke at this point is that contrasting 'public' and 'private' spheres. The workings of some institutional areas are held to be the concern of many groups (although some are disenfranchised) and there is public discussion about them. But, in other spheres, they are not held to warrant much attention and discussion is suppressed or deflected into private nooks and crannies. In modern western societies it has been held traditionally that only men have a voice in 'public spheres' (such as the economy and polity) whereas those spheres in which women's concerns are considered to be dominant warrant little attention. This is slowly changing.

Another very important framework stands behind the nation-state (and the national economy) which is so often assumed by social analysts to be the most appropriate context for their work. Over a couple of decades now, Immanuel Wallerstein has built a 'world-systems' framework (e.g. Hopkins and Wallerstein 1982, as illustrated in Chapter 2). This approach has strong Marxist influences, but has also been strongly influenced by the Annales school of French social historians. The world-systems approach argues that the internal unity and significance of nation-states has been considerably exaggerated. Rather, since the sixteenth century at least, the various European (and later other) nations have been embedded within a wider and expanding world-system which has been girded by flows of trade, capital, culture and people. The possibilities open to particular countries, regions or even individual enterprises are very considerably (often quite overwhelmingly) shaped by their position in relation to the world-system. These positions are discussed in terms of three or four main zones:

- the metropolitan core;
- the semi-periphery;
- the periphery; and
- unincorporated areas.

The metropolitan core is at the centre of the system and ensures that the system is organised for it to obtain the best value. The core has been traditionally involved with manufacture and service provision and is politically and militarily powerful. The core is not, however, laced together by political mechanisms, although there may be significant coordinating arrangements (e.g. the OECD) and often there is a 'hegemonic' state among those states in the core countries, which then becomes the 'leader of the orchestra' (e.g. the role played over much of this century by the USA). Instead, the power of the core over the rest of the world-system is wielded, rather more cheaply in terms of the resources required, mainly by economic means. Empires are much more expensive because more direct state coordination is required.

The semi-periphery mediates between core and periphery, both exploiting the periphery, but also being exploited by the core. Semi-periphery countries may also be vulnerable to being pushed and pulled by the rather different sets of forces affecting them from both core and periphery. As a result, some of their institutions may be quite volatile.

Finally, the periphery is the rim of countries whose unprocessed resources are extracted by the core and who serve as the relatively powerless markets for core products. This theory has, of course, been expanded beyond this bald treatment to protect itself from the many difficulties that its detractors have held up.

The analyst of any social structure should bear in mind what the influence might be of the relevant institutional environment in which it is placed. Few sociologists study institutional areas in their own right. Nevertheless, any sociological analysis must be sensitive to the particular cultural values embedded in institutional areas and their structural configurations. It is an area of sociological investigation in need of much attention.

SOCIAL CONSTRUCTION PROCESSES (CONSTRUCTING THE BOXES)

Social structures are almost never built anew from the ground up. On the other hand, nor can they readily be seen as fragile frameworks that are freshly reconstructed each day. It is more reasonable to take an intermediate position to draw attention to those social processes of social construction which provide the more or less stable frameworks that shape everyday social life, and which also legitimate and bolster it. The main framework around which social structures are built is cultural: it is the set of 'constitutional' ideas held about how that social structure is to be put together. This cognitive and moral framework then provides the boundaries and sets the terms within which the social structure actually works. However, this point does not imply that this shared cultural framework is necessarily the most important component in the workings of the social structure.

This set of processes has not been studied by any particular approach within sociology. A general framework was sketched by Berger and Luckmann (1966; see above in Chapter 3), which provides some general guidance. More detailed and empirically-related material relevant to the processes of structure-building can be cobbled together from several diverse sources:

107

- Studies of the sources of organisational arrangements from a 'radical' economic sociology viewpoint concerned to repudiate the more common argument that organisational structure is determined by 'technological imperatives'.
- Studies, from a 'Bourdieu-ian' approach, of the social construction of a new social category.
- Tilly's concept of a 'contention repertoire'.
- Insights gleaned from the application of symbolic interactionist and social representational approaches to macro-sociological issues.

There have been several very interesting studies of the social construction of social structures. In her historical study of the US steel industry, Kathleen Stone (1974) was able to show that, between 1880 and 1920, the then-present job-structure of the internal organisation of steel mills developed. In the classical mode of organisation of steel plants, skilled workers controlled the production process through a structure which comprised a strong union of these skilled workers, a contract system, a sliding scale for wages and an apprentice-helper arrangement. However, the employers, who controlled the capital, wished to expand production to take advantage of burgeoning market opportunities without providing the skilled workers with a substantial share of the profits that would accrue. They were able to introduce labour-saving technology and wrest control of the production process from the skilled workers. The new technology was used to convert both skilled workers and heavy labourers into semi-skilled machine operators. The painfully-developed information held by the skilled workers was no longer essential. The owners also developed institutions to further control the production process, involving wage incentive schemes, promotion hierarchies and welfare programmes. The roles of foremen and managers changed as well, and the whole apparatus was organised around the managerial (rather than worker) control of the knowledge involved with the steel production.

Stone enunciates the following conclusions:

1 Technology, by itself, did not create today's labour system: technology merely defined the realm of possibilities.
2 The development of hierarchy in the labour force was not a response to the increased complexity of jobs, but rather a device to counter the increased simplicity and homogeneity of jobs.
3 The issues of how work shall be organised, how jobs shall be defined, and how workers shall be paid are points of conflict and class struggle between workers and employers. The structures that emerge can only be understood in those terms. Any explanation based on impersonal market forces or natural economic laws misses the actual historical development.
4 The division of labour of today that separates mental work from physical work is an artificial and unnecessary division that only serves to maintain the power of employers over their workers.

108

5 The labour market structures that were developed in the early part of this century under the banner of 'scientific management' have lasted, in refined forms, until today. No labour movement or reform group has yet developed successful means for overthrowing them and establishing a more rational system for getting work done.

A more widely framed study by Boltanski (1987) traces through the development in France of a social group that is termed 'cadres', which very broadly corresponds to the 'new middle class' (often including technical personnel such as engineers). The complexity and fluidity of this group is reflected in the study, which thereby resists easy summary. Boltanski places at the centre of his study the collective social conception held by cadres, and he traces the development of this conception over time. At the core of the socially shared conception is a 'role-model' group of cadres with business school backgrounds and computer-linked occupations, together with similar high prestige connotations. However, this image only connects partially with the reality of the wider social grouping. So it is clear that aspirations are as important as present realities to the wider range of people that identify with being a cadre. Boltanski also shows how this social category has been propelled by organisational activities and historical circumstances. His study (and especially the conclusion) emphasises the contingent way in which such social categories develop, and the complexities and subtleties of the relations between individuals and their groupings. In particular, representatives and spokes-persons can be crucial in shaping the development of a social category.

Tilly (e.g. 1981) has developed the study of 'repertoires of contention' as part of fine-grained research into social movements accompanying long-term trends in modernising societies. He is interested in showing how the possibilities for action in any group are shaped by the range of possibilities that they consider are available to them.

Any group who has a common interest in collective action also acquires a shared repertoire of routines among which it makes a choice when the occasion for pursuing an interest or a grievance arises. The metaphor calls attention to the limited number of performances available to any particular group at a given time, to the learned character of these performances, to the possibility of innovation and improvisation within the limits set by the existing means, to the likelihood that not only the actors but also the objects of their action are aware of the character of the drama that is unfolding, and finally to the element of collective choice that enters into the events which outsiders call riots, distortions, disturbances and protests.

(Tilly 1981: 161)

In eighteenth-century repertoires, the most distinctive forms of revolt were the anti-tax rebellion, the food riot and the concerted invasion of fields or forests.

Whereas in the nineteenth century, from the 1830s on, the repertoire featured special-purpose associations often aimed at sustained pressure on the polity, expressed in the forms of strikes, demonstrations, electoral rallies and formal meetings. This repertoire largely has continued into the present. Each repertoire can be shown to be rooted in the particular social structure of the period.

While Tilly has developed this conception in relation to the framing of public protests, my point is that this approach can be used far more widely. In all areas of society, social structures are constrained by the culturally-available imagination of its members. We live in those social structures we can imagine. For example, Benedict Anderson has argued this most decisively in relation to the rise of different conceptions of the nation-state (Anderson 1983). The role of repertoires seems most obvious in areas of experimentation such as residential arrangements (e.g. communes) and work arrangements (e.g. worker participation). Study of the availability and usage of repertoires for social organisation is always important.

Several other points have been adduced by those studying social structure from social interactionist or culturological perspectives. In these approaches, attention is directed towards the ideologies which shape people's under-standings of their social environment, the symbols which are the vehicles of these meanings and the rituals which act these out, while mobilising supporting sentiments. One significant programme has become organised around the concept of the 'negotiated order' (see Claggett 1988; Denzin 1992; Hall 1987; Maines 1991). This approach recognises that social life is governed by shared meanings, but emphasises the complex and fragile way in which such shared meanings are put together. It is clear that most social structures are wreathed in layers of symbolism and studying this is vital to understanding how the social structure operates. These conceptual frameworks are, in part, constitutive of social structures through the cognitive infrastructure they lay down, and in addition they are highly significant in providing legitimation for the way social structures are organised.

There are many studies of various aspects within this set of 'constitutive' social processes (as well as a plethora of programmatic statements), but this is yet another area of study where more coherence needs to be achieved.

PEOPLING PROCESSES (FILLING THE BOXES)

Once (as it were) the empty places in social structures are set up, they can be filled with people. Further processes deal with how the people that are recruited for positions are then handled in that position: their sustenance, promotion and disposal! The types of people who come to occupy a social structure can then, by virtue of their own characteristics, have social consequences, since they may well endeavour to shape the structure 'in their own image'. I should repeat here a warning made elsewhere in this book: peopling should not be seen as a process other than *analytically* separated from other structural processes. It should surprise no-one that social structures are very often designed (not necessarily at all consciously) with a particular social category in mind.

Much interest in peopling centres on how people are recruited into positions. The most basic distinction is between recruitment on ascriptive criteria and recruitment on achievement criteria. In ascription frames, recruitment is fixed by pre-set biological or kinship characteristics, whereas in achievement frames, wider bases of selection criteria are possible.

Especially for paid-work positions, recruitment is largely structured on a social class basis, albeit mediated by the effect of schooling and educational credentials. Gender, ethnic and other effects are also strong. Bourdieu has pointed out that this social class basis for recruitment involves the cultural capital obtained from people's home environments, reinforced by the way schooling (largely captured by middle-class intellectuals) is organised to amplify the effects of class-based cultural capitals. The very style and ambiance of education institutions operate to reinforce these processes. There is a huge literature on this, partly in the sociology of work, but particularly in the sociology of education.

Attention also needs to be addressed to the mechanisms through which people may come to hear of jobs to apply for. In his classic network study, Granovetter (1973) was able to show that, for many, the information which yielded a job offer came from relatively remote and chance linkages. After all, the information scanning range of close contacts is more likely to be narrow and overlap with the information horizon of the job-seeker themselves, whereas the far-flung nature of the network immensely broadens its scanning range.

Beyond workplace situations, an even wider array of recruitment mechanisms may come into play. Marriage can be taken as a somewhat different example.

Once people are in place they may be motivated, instructed, cooled-out, monitored, supervised, sanctioned, rewarded and perhaps placed within a promotional ladder or other schemes for handling their progress. Again, study of these processes is attended to in several literatures including the sociology of work, but also of all other social institutions. By now, much has been learned about the likely effects of different schema for surveillance, reward and punishments. For example, piece rates tend to encourage more vigorous work performance, but often at the cost of higher accident rates and attenuation of social relationships.

Once places have been filled with people, the compositional pattern resulting can have its own effects. For example, in various community studies, the question has been posed about the extent to which a locality affects the people living within it (e.g. Gans 1968). One major influence is clearly the effect of the physical and spatial environment and another is the particular history of the area. However, an important point is that, beyond these obvious comparisons, many of the differences between communities arise precisely out of the mix they contain of different social categories of people. A community of middle class people is likely to operate in quite a different way than one composed of working-class people; a retirement community will be different than a 'nappy valley' of young newly-weds. Compositional features of a community can have quite a direct effect in their own right. Of course, this point applies to social structures other than communities as well.

Peter Blau (e.g. 1977; Blau and Schwartz 1984) has developed an ambitious theory of the effects of social compositions. After working in the Mertonian case-study approach to organisations (on exchange theory, inter-generational occupational mobility studies and more formal organisational studies), he turned in the mid-1970s to the formal development of a 'primitive theory' of macro-structure. This provides a clearer specification of Durkheim's concerns about the consequences of division of labour for the pattern of social integration. However, for Blau, the 'division of labour' involves the considerably wider conception of the composition of the pre-given social structure, and any interest in the overall level of social integration is deflected into the narrower issue of the patterns of social interaction between the groups comprising that social structure. So, the scope of Blau's concern nestles inside Durkheim's wider reach. The main image for the development of his approach comes from Simmel's concepts of concentric and crosscutting circles (both Simmel and Blau were reviewed in Chapter 3; see also Garnsey 1981).

The key to his theory is that any social structure has 'structural parameters' which are built up from the characteristics of aggregates of its members. These then form aggregate-level opportunity-structures which, in turn, may constrain or provide opportunities for individual behaviour, especially behaviour which involves interaction across (or within) the social boundaries indicated by these parameters. An obvious example is that one finds it hard to meet an Eskimo in a town without Eskimos – or, rather more realistically, that one's chances of meeting an Eskimo tend to be shaped by the proportion of Eskimos in your place of residence.

Blau argues that there are two main types of social background characteristic, and his typology is based on the measurement properties involved with the social distributions of each of these. On the one hand, there are 'nominal' type characteristics where the population is divided up into several bounded groups (e.g. ethnicity), while on the other there are 'graduated' parameters which have interval level-of-measurement type characteristics (e.g. income or education). Aggregating these characteristics across population groupings leads to the structural properties of heterogeneity (in relation to nominal parameters) and inequality (in relation to nominal level parameters). The last step in Blau's strategy is to show that it is the intersection of heterogeneity and inequality which is most significant in affecting the overall operation of society.

Most recently, Blau (1994) has interrelated several areas of study (including organisations and inter-generational occupational mobility within a wider framework) that deserves consideration of how historical changes have affected social structures. Centre-stage is still given to structural parameters. This approach has been tested across a wide range of phenomena and has often been shown to produce useful predictions. Blau's approach is able to reveal some of the ways in which people's involvement with others is shaped by the opportunity-structures in which they live or operate. It is an inventive use of available data to point out the inherent structural features within a social structure. Criticisms of it neglecting the subjective (e.g. Giddens 1984) or of being partially tautological (e.g. Porpora 1987) strike me as damning only if this is taken to be the only approach possible in sociology.

However, Blau's classification of types of parameters is, in my view, deficient. He slips from focusing on more inherent qualities by attending, instead, to 'measurement properties'. In particular, target-groups or client-groups (e.g. ethnic minorities, women) are usually identified in terms of nominal categories, whereas 'resources' (inputs?) or 'rewards' (outputs?) are typically measured on interval scales (albeit often grouped). I suggest that, in developing the thrust of his theory, Blau's conceptualisation has slipped into measurement terms, and that to return to characteristics of groups and their resources is a formulation which would improve his theory. (This reworking also deals with the otherwise awkward point that age, which is clearly a social background characteristic, is interval, whereas some resources/rewards may very well be nominal.) The scope of Blau's programme has also had the effect of invigorating methodological interest in modelling 'multi-level structures' (e.g. DiPreto and Forristal 1994).

A final point is that it can be useful to think of any particular social structure as recruiting from 'primordial' social structures (such as households and families) or, more generally, the aggregate members of a population. As Parsons and orthodox economists see it, households provide labour for firms in exchange for obtaining the goods and services purchased from peoples' pay-packets. (This overlaps the 'public–private' boundaries mentioned earlier.) People and social units from these primordial structures will have their own strategies and approaches to the way they are prepared to 'people' the social structure. In modern societies, family/households are important units, which are usually the seat of major decisions about the commitment of resources. Families often have more or less planned strategies for relating to various other social structures in their environment. For example, trade-offs will be made between household duties as opposed to income-generating opportunities, and between educational investment (especially in children) and immediate income-generation. The peopling of structural positions involves complex plays between various social actors and social units.

Much of the flow of people into the slots provided by social structures is controlled by those who set them up or run them in the first place. On the other hand, those who come to fill them adapt various long-term strategies and short-term tactics in the way they 'use' their position. It is in the peopling of social structures where much of the interplay between ordinary people and controllers of structures takes place.

RESOURCE DISTRIBUTIONS (PRODUCING FROM THE BOXES)

Social positions are assigned tasks to do and, accordingly, are allocated resources to carry out these tasks. They also are involved, as Marx would remind us, in actually producing resources (e.g. commodities). Also, as a surge of more recent research interest indicates, they are also involved in consumption. Yet, it is strange how the pages of the literature of sociology seem often inhabited by quite vacuous social structures, which do little and have little to do it with.

What can be used as a resource is defined by the culture concerned. Different cultures may have considerably different conceptions of the use of the same array of potential resources. For example, oil is central to the running of modern capitalist societies, and yet may have been regarded as merely a curious seepage by other cultures. Groupings within a social structure may vary in their discernment of alternative uses for resources. Sewell (1992) points out that this social distribution of the alternative potential use of resources ought to be built into sociological understandings of resources.

Resources, as such, are therefore often regarded as falling outside social structure. They are things used by the social structure. In the first place, resources are the immediately useable aspects of the environment the social structure sits within, especially the natural environment. (The more diffuse aspects of the natural environment presumably provide more general assistance, e.g. in providing a physical stage.) In addition, people can be beset by any of a catalogue of dangers or risks: 'anti-resources' such as wind, fire, storm, earthquake. The hard physicality of some resources may have a direct effect on social behaviour.

However, *physical* resources are but one form of a wider class. In addition, social structures create 'social' resources, as a product of the activities of their members. Giddens has identified 'authoritative resources' as those which offer power levers over other people. Bourdieu extends this with the term 'cultural capital' and the even wider conception of 'social capital'. He draws useful distinctions between such aspects of 'capital' as the extent to which they can be institutionalised and to what extent they can be appropriated by individuals (e.g. with educational capital in the form of credentials). Philosopher Karl Popper refers to the whole cultural heritage which people build and then live in as 'World 3', with its own (albeit constructed) autonomous reality.

Economists have developed some distinctions about different types of resources. As opposed to the usual commodity of capitalism which is a 'private good', other resources are described as 'public goods'. These differ from private goods in terms of whether the use of a good exhausts it, and/or whether access to

114

the benefits of the good can be kept private. Sunsets, for example, are clearly a public good, although access to a gorgeous uninterrupted view of them (accompanied by chilled champagne on a warm unpolluted beach!) may not be. There are many intermediate categories, especially where goods have 'externalities': where their use by one person has effects on other people. That goods have beneficial externalities, which people can enjoy but cannot be readily charged for, allows 'free-riders' to benefit. In fact, very few goods are 'purely' private, perhaps just household retail items such as bread and butter. Another distinction which can be important for distinguishing between different types of resources is whether or not they are renewable (e.g. hydro-electric power) or non-renewable (e.g. coal-generated electricity), to give examples relating to physical resources.

These distinctions have important implications relating to the operation of markets, as well as the social groupings in these markets. Classic markets work best with pure private goods and progressively are less and less able to handle goods with more 'public' characteristics. Public goods are more likely to be handled through non-market mechanisms such as rationing or direct state control. Sometimes, as in contemporary welfare state reform, attempts are made to set up 'quasi-markets' in which coupons or other money-substitutes are artificially provided to enable the goods to be allocated other than on a rationing basis. In a market society, public goods are usually not handled very well and this is likely to lead to 'private wealth but public squalor' (to use Galbraith's evocative phrase).

How are resources allocated and acquired? In some part, resources are allocated 'rationally' (in the eyes of the authorities distributing the resources) to enable people in particular positions to carry out those tasks. This type of bland assertion, though, suppresses the often vigorous processes of competition and conflict between and within social units. Within any firm there will be struggles between different departments for more resources, although there may be quite different types of resources which are struggled over. For example, a common conflict is between a marketing or sales department which wishes to serve the interests of the firm's customers, and the production side which is sensitive to the internal limitations of the production technology. In markets, firms compete for market share. Similarly, nations compete to keep up their standards of living and their ability to beat the goods produced in other nations in terms of price or standard.

In the same way, the distribution of resources (once they have been rendered ready for use) as rewards is also seen as rational in the eyes of the authorities responsible for their distribution. Certainly, ideological justifications to legitimate income distributions argue this. But as with the pattern of resource allocation, the pattern of reward allocation is the outcome of contemporaneous and historical struggles among various social groupings. Certainly, resources are often distributed along social class lines and other lines of social cleavage such as gender and ethnicity are important. A host of empirical studies have been carried out on income distribution. To a considerable extent the rewards are related to the earning-capacity of individuals, which comes from those of their characteristics which are valued on the job-market. But in addition, sociologists have pointed out that much is shaped by the opportunity structures which they face, which they may influence barely at all.

The Mertonian concept of 'opportunity-structure' is a general-purpose framework often deployed by sociologists to indicate the ways in which groups differ in terms of their legitimate access to resources. For example, Merton argued that deviance was particularly generated in those groups where, despite a shared cultural pressure to do well, these groups lacked the ready access to achieve occupational or financial success. Such a propensity might be further reinforced when people in this position had access to an 'illegitimate' opportunity-structure in which the means of deviance was available to them. Opportunity-structures do not, however, explain everything: Rubenstein (1992) has gently criticised sociologists for often over-emphasising the explanatory power of opportunity structures at the cost of not also investigating the social characteristics of those involved.

As an area of separate theoretically-sophisticated investigation, resource distribution processes seem understudied (an exception is Blalock 1990). Although there is a long tradition of investigation of poverty, income distribution, wealth distribution and the like, this seems only broadly attended to in social theory, beyond the general treatment this area receives in discussions of social class, gender and ethnicity.

SOCIAL CHANGE/TRANSFORMATION PROCESSES (CHANGING THE BOXES)

Too much can be made of the distinction between the normal ebb and flow of the day-to-day social process and more definite changes in arrangements. Often the distinction is quite arbitrary and, in general, change is best seen as lying on a continuum between normality and radical discontinuity. After all: *plus ça change, plus ça reste la même chose.* On the other hand, there are social processes which directly and consciously involve the reshaping – or the attempted reshaping or, indeed, defence – of existing structural arrangements. In order not to slight such processes, separate attention is needed.

Early theories of social change and revolution often focused on the collective behaviour of riots and disorderly assemblies which are often the human face of turbulent social change. Much (often essentially conservative) social commentary on these collective events stressed their irrational, sentiment-laden, 'mob psychology' nature and the regression into animal-like and imitative behaviour of those involved.

The more recent response from sociologists has tended to draw a much wider picture involving societal breakdown, mounting social stress and other broad social conditions as favouring change and ferment. A search was

116

mounted for *social* causes of stress and disruption. This was often put together as a 'hydraulic' model in which it was argued that the greater the depths of frustration and deprivation, the higher the likelihood of revolt. This was sometimes seen as a Dukheimian approach (see Tilly 1984). However, this does not fit with much empirical evidence in several respects. First, it is not so much *absolute* deprivation as *relative* deprivation that leads to frustration. But more importantly, it requires some skills, resources and social organisation to protest, so that a drive for social change is more likely to be launched from somewhere higher up in the stratificational order than down below. Indeed, extreme deprivation may lead more to withdrawal and chaos than to violent action.

The array of social movements of the 1960s precipitated a much closer look at the mechanics of social change. The civil rights, women's, environmental, peace, gay/lesbian and other social movements were all struggling for success under the bright lights of media publicity. Reflection on the comparative successes and failures of these movements seemed a fertile ground for developing a sociology of social movements. More recent writing in these areas has sometimes noted the links in their ideas to the enunciated strategy and tactics for fostering social change advocated by social change activists and theorists such as Lenin, Trotsky, Mao and Alinsky. (This is part of a two-way trade in ideas between the lay world and analysts.)

A broad approach labelled 'resource mobilisation theory' (RMT) developed. One stream of this approach works at a social psychological level, making the assumption that, in fact, involvement in social change is rational and explaining people's involvement in terms of their incentives and costs (as in the broader REM model). At the membership level, the role of social network links in recruiting people and ensuring their continued participation is seen as crucial. (See Buechler 1993; Morris and Mueller 1992.)

The other stream of RMT works at an organisational level, rather more as seen from the viewpoint of a social movement leader. It is therefore concerned with resources, recruitment, strategies and tactics, ideology and communication, not to forget organisational arrangements. In this approach, a distinction is made between the 'Social Movement Organisation' (SMO) or organisations in the vanguard of the conflict, and the long tail of the more or less almost-passive support which good causes often receive – or evil ones for that matter. It is not enough, of course, to concentrate on just the social movement itself – the wider social environment, competitors and counter-movements have also to be taken into account. In addition, the needs of the organisation itself, just to maintain itself as an organisation, can begin to cut into, or even deflect, the drive for change.

Resource mobilisation theory can be seen as a broad framework within which historical understandings about social movements can be accumulated and particular theories about social movements can be tested. In more specificity, these analysts have argued that:

(a) movement actions are rational, adaptive responses to the costs and rewards of different lines of action;

(b) the basic goals of movements are defined by conflicts of interest built into institutionalised power relations;

(c) the grievances generated by such conflicts are sufficiently ubiquitous that the formation and mobilisation of movements depends on changes in resources, group organisation, and opportunities for collective action;

(d) centralised, formally structured movement organisations are more typical of model social movements and more effective at mobilising resources and mounting sustained challenges than decentralised, informal movement structures; and

(e) the success of movements is largely determined by strategic factors and political processes in which they become enmeshed.

(Jenkins 1983: 528)

More recently, a European-based approach, often labelled 'New Social Movement' (NSM) theory, has arisen to partly complement and partly challenge the slightly older US-based approach. The NSM theorists are much more concerned with the societal framework within which social change movements are launched and, in particular, about the cultural and ideological messages they carry. A distinction is drawn between the older social movements for change, which are seen as strongly class-linked, and newer social movements which are seen as reflecting rather different sectional interests.

The more recent peace, environmental etc. movements are seen to reflect a different set of values about society than those held in the mainstream of that society. This, in turn, can lead to new organisational forms being adopted by them which better reflect these values. This new ideology tends to de-emphasise the material wealth concerns of the older agenda in contrast to 'quality of life' concerns, such as those relating to the physical environment. NSMs also tend to be egalitarian in terms of their political philosophy, stressing widespread political participation. Thus, NSMs confront various of the central values and structural arrangements of modern societies: materialism, traditional moral values, as well as class, patriarchy and racism. The very diffuseness of their social background can, in turn, lead to a marked fluidity of membership involvement (since involvement is not sanctioned by any social solidarity). NSMs are likely to be quite media-conscious and can use the media to appeal directly to supporters without building up large organisational support. Protest activities may be carefully staged and, indeed, may have to be as they cannot deliver a solid steady block of voting support that is needed for involvement in traditional politics.

The NSM approach focuses on different aspects of social movements, but does not necessarily require a totally new sociological approach. It can be seen to blend in with the older resource mobilisation approach. In turn, both approaches can be seen to draw on a variety of theoretical models covering organisations, inter-organisational fields, networks, power etc. that are available within the general stocks of theoretical knowledge in sociology.

Revolutions

The sociology of revolution partially overlaps and partially extends the more general study of social change. 'Social revolutions are rapid, basic transformations of a society's state and class structures; and they are accompanied and in part carried through by class-based revolts from below' (Skocpol 1979: 4). Because of their dramatic nature and their large-scale effects, revolutions must be firmly placed on the agenda of any sociological approach, as they can be seen as providing a crucial empirical test for any general theoretical approach.

The current 'generation' of thinking about revolutions is based on the experience of what can be identified (Foran 1993, citing Goldstone) as three previous generations. The first generation of work involved 'natural histories' of revolutions, which remained as essentially historically descriptive, as few explicit comparisons were drawn and theoretical explanations remained inherent in the structure of the narrative. A second generation of studies in the 1960s used functionalist theories of modernisation and the 'hydraulic' model of deprivation and tended to be too vague to be very successful.

It was the structural analyses of the third generation of theorising (building on the work of Barrington Moore and Wolfe) that began to build up more sociologically sophisticated theories of revolution. In the third generation theories, a variety of economic and/or economic structural forces were seen as setting up the conditions under which revolutions might be possible and the conditions under which they might be carried through. The range which the agency revolutionaries (and others) might exert was seen as narrow. Revolutions are seen as arising out of particular historical circumstances created out of the changing relations between social entities such as various classes, the state, other states and so forth. For example, Skocpol particularly emphasised the autonomous role of the state and its weakening or collapse as central in leading to possibilities for revolutions.

Since the 1980s, analysts interested in this area have been working within the broad framework sketched out by the earlier theorists. Theorists are employing a wide array of elements in their explanations, including complex understandings of social structures, political apparatuses and the economy, relations with other states and culture, as well as providing room for the agency of revolutionaries and regime-defenders. Quite flexible and complex combinations of elements are seen as necessary in providing any adequate, and thus 'conjunctural', explanations. Wider ranges of cases are explored through careful comparison. Clearly, the approaches are increasingly sophisticated, although the increasing complexity in turn leads to difficulties in consolidating overall theories with sufficient internal consistency.

In these various aspects, it could be said that the field of studying revolutions reflects the overall state of theory in relation to social structure. However, I sense that a difference lies in the much closer and more continual attention to issues of structural explanation among analysts of revolutions, which is aided by their much more sharply defined focus of interest. Social analysts who concentrate on less momentous topics may be more neglectful of social structural issues.

However, neither the study of social movements nor revolutions exhausts the range of investigations required in broad processes of change and struggle between social groupings.

LIFE COURSE ASPECTS (MOVING THROUGH THE BOXES)

The power of a life course perspective comes from showing the extent to which people's present attitudes and behaviour is explained by their past positions in the social structure (or by the line of their trajectory through the social structure). This viewpoint on social structures has not yet settled-down into widely-shared and highly-developed systematic frameworks, but it brims with many exciting developments (see e.g. Cohen 1987; Dex 1991; Elder 1994; George 1993; O'Rand and Krecker 1990).

It is not surprising that this area of the study of social structure has only recently developed since it is difficult enough to study social structure at any one time, let alone have sufficient understanding to conceptualise how the whole structure both changes and reproduces itself over time. Some of the methodological difficulties are also intractable. In principle, at least, one must envisage two time-slices of social structure and then map the linkages between these two:

• The social source or origin.
• The social destination or outcome.
• The social aspects of the social change group (e.g. generation).

In this perspective, the analyses focus on ordered patterns of change, and how these both:

• are based on prior social structure; and
• effect subsequent social structure.

Some of the complexity comes, therefore, from the multiple viewpoints from which social trajectories can be viewed. They may be seen from the perspective of the situation out of which they arose, the situation which resulted, from the changing situation of those changing, or against the background of those not contemporaneously involved in change.

In this section, I explore different conceptualisations of the structured ways in which members of a society move through its array of social structural positions. In doing so they, of course, tend to also change the social structure they are moving through, although the emphasis in life-course accounts lies in holding the structure constant while examining the progress of individuals within it. (Another important view of social structure over time is to analyse social structural changes, which has been reviewed in the previous section).

Study of social trajectories is riddled with methodological complexities, to which life-course theorists also need to be alert. One of the most important distinctions which must be made is that between those in an age-group, and a generation or cohort, at any one time – without a longitudinal research design, it is impossible to separate what about any age-group is due to its current situation in the age-structure, and what is due to its own unique history as a generation (White 1973). What 60-year-olds think or do may be because that is what 60-year-olds in any age-structure think or do, or it may be some reflection of the historical experience of a particular bunch of 60-year-olds.

Another methodological problem arises in developing measures of change-groupings, since they can be examined from the perspective of before, after or during. But if there are methodological difficulties which arise from the tracing of a grouping between two time-slices, these are multiplied very considerably in endeavouring to trace a change-grouping across multiple time-slices or, indeed, over a whole life-course.

Analyses of social trajectories differ in terms of their time-scale. One boundary that forms a useful marking point is that of a life-time: in a few cases approximating the biblical injunction of 'three score years and ten'. Some studies are potentially longer-term than this, such as those which trace the extent to which the features of one generation are 'reproduced' in the following generation. However, these are likely to focus more on the approximate twenty-year period separating generations. (In inter-generational studies, the comparison is often made between a respondent and features of their parents when they were at secondary school: e.g. age 15.) On the other hand, other temporal studies may attempt to catch fleeting moments: such as the analyses of conversational turn-taking often employed in conversational analyses.

While many studies of social trajectories emphasise the smooth flow and long-term consistency of social trajectories, other studies focus on discontinuities and the effects of these on life-courses and contemporary situations. Such interruptions include deaths, major injuries or illnesses, mental breakdown, unemployment and other shocks, either to persons themselves or to someone close to them. In 'life events' analysis, it is assumed that individuals and social units are subject to occasional (perhaps regular and frequent) social shocks and that these contribute to stress with which they invariously cope.

Life courses also needed to be viewed from the viewpoint of the social structure itself. At any one time, when a social structure is analytically frozen for viewing (as in a single camera shot), it must be remembered that, in fact, any social structure is composed of various social groups and individuals each with different trajectories, starting points and destinations. Often the vectors of this past and future movement are not captured by social analyses which concentrate solely on the present. Differentiating between the variety of groupings, each on their different trajectories, may reveal a rather different understanding of social change.

Yet, on the other hand, it may be that much of the micro-movement over time cancels itself out. It may well prove to be ironic that the huge effort which may go into tracking many trajectories may yield minimal reward: the myriad complexities of social trajectories may result in social structures which, nevertheless, very substantially reproduce themselves. Somehow, out of all the micro-chaos, a majestically stable unchanging social world may endlessly reproduce itself. However, this is not the likely outcome of all studies of social change.

So far, I have addressed general issues relating to all kinds of life course approach, and can now focus on more specific frameworks. Various of these can be located within a sequence of topics which might be covered, such as studies of

- social frameworks for handling change;
- objective patterns of change;
- subjective experiences of change;
- sources (determinants) of change;
- concomitants of change; and
- consequences of change.

Most social structures are organised to deal with changes in their personnel and circumstances. As role analysts have pointed out, roles are often organised in role-sequences, statuses in status-sequences, and status-sets in status-set sequences.

The succession of statuses occurring with sufficient frequency as to be socially patterned will be designated as a status-sequence, as in the case, for example, of the statuses successively occupied by a medical student, intern, resident and independent medical practitioner. In much the same sense, of course, we can observe sequences of role-sets and status-sets (Merton 1968: 424). Such sequences are not only recognised and expected, but are also often governed by 'socially expected durations' concerning the timing of each phase. An example of this is that of a 'lame duck' politician, after being defeated in the polls but not yet replaced by the victor. One mechanism tying such sequences together is 'anticipatory socialisation' in which people may orientate themselves to views and behaviour associated with subsequent stages.

There may be a temptation to concentrate more on paths of upward movement, whereas downward progressions are also important to study. After all, mechanisms are needed for the firing or demoting of people, almost as much as those required for their hiring and promotion. And as Goffman reminds us, ways of 'cooling out' those in these difficulties may be preferable to avoid too much negative impact on them.

Major portions of culture are orientated around providing meaning and a social context of social support through involvement in rituals around the time of the various break-points: birth, adolescence, adulthood, marriage, death etc. 'Rites de passage' serve to shore up the uncertainties and risks associated with people's movement between stages.

Beyond the handling of changes of individuals or groupings of individuals through the social pattern, social structures may also have relatively formal mechanisms for handling adjustment to other sources of social change. As Etzioni (1968) has indicated, at one extreme societies may be quite self-directive, being capable of monitoring their environment, mobilising appropriate redesign suggestions and implementing these through mechanisms akin to planning and social change agencies.

A range of quite different types of study have been concerned with the patterns of people's movement within the social structure. Perhaps the most arduous producers of basic information about change are the demographers through their cohort analyses of births, deaths, migration, divorce etc. of different age-sex groupings. Another important type of study are those which trace inter-generational occupational mobility between parents and sons or daughters (notably Blau and Duncan 1967). This type of study is vital in understanding how open or closed a social formation is to change over time: a 'closed' society sharply reproduces in children their parent's social position, whereas a more 'open' society allows room for individual talent and other social factors to result in changed social arrangements between generations. This makes the study of occupational mobility of very considerable theoretical interest, although in practice the similarities of findings across divergent contexts seems to reduce the excitement that this type of study seems to promise.

As well as studying the transmission of occupations, studies have examined the socially-structured patterns through which this transmission is shaped, through mediating variables such as schooling, parental household resources, sibling order, military service, first job and so forth. These can be summarised in concepts such as the pattern of 'status-attainment'. In addition, the transmission of a huge range of other values and characteristics between generations is possible.

Studies may look much more closely at the complex twists and turns of sequences of social positions. For example, the work histories or residential histories of people can be immensely varied. Moreover, these are complicated further by the different exposures people have as a result of their age or their differential involvement: as a result, the histories of older people are likely to be more varied than those of younger. Sifting through such rich data in order to yield clear-cut patterns is not easy, especially with little in the way of theoretical guidance.

The types of study noted so far are those which tend to emphasise the objective patterns of life-course changes. In addition, some studies emphasise the more qualitative and subjective aspects. One important concept that can be used to guide this type of study is that of a 'moral career' as suggested by Becker (1970). In this approach, analysts are sensitised to the different stages through which people meaningfully commit themselves to a particular role. For example, a marijuana smoker has to learn not just how to smoke, but how to do so in the style to which they are supposed to grow accustomed. A criminal may be so labelled by police or courts, and then may get to accept this label of themselves, which then creates them as a criminal.

A wider application of this approach is that of the 'life-history' where aspects of all of the above are combined: together with locating the person within their own wider, but changing, social contexts. In a life-history, the sequences through which a person has lived are reconstructed, particularly in the subjective terms with which that person sees their own biography.

Not only do social structures differ in the extent to which they propel social movement (their degree of 'openness' vs. 'closedness'), but there are also differences in terms of the social consequences of different patterns of social trajectory. It may be that the extent and the pace of change each have different effects. Certainly, they will have different effects under different social conditions. However, there are as yet too few studies of social-structures-in-change for clear-cut conclusions to emerge.

Some of the more important contributions to sociology have been accomplished by scholars working within one or other of several 'life course' approaches. These have yielded a close-textured picture of how the often-smooth surface pattern of a society is produced out of very complex across-time arrangements. A difficult agenda of complex methodological issues has been posed and is being tackled, although the carrying out of across-time studies remains challenging. However, the variety of different research traditions working alongside each other could usefully be compacted into broader more comprehensive frameworks.

SPATIAL AND TEMPORAL CONTEXTS

In recent social theory, there has been a particular concentration on the spatial and temporal dimensions to social life. This includes a fascination with the ways in which, at the personal level, social interaction is no longer dependent on face-to-face modes of communication and, at a more general level, at the burgeoning spatial scale of social entities and how social power and influence can be 'projected' across progressively further distances. Similarly, there is growing attention to the ways in which experiences, memories and traditions influence later events. The spatial view of the social world is accompanied with a heightened concern about the ways in which the physical features of environment relate to people's bodies and identities.

The historical view of the social world is accompanied by a heightened concern with contingencies, accidents and inter-relations. It is ironic that, in times when the tyranny of distance and time is most readily overcome by technology, there is a growing theoretical concern with spatial and temporal aspects of social structures.

The difficulty for social analysts is knowing how to incorporate these general theoretical concerns into working understandings and procedures. It is not even clear whether separate approaches are needed, or whether spatial and temporal aspects can be adequately addressed as aspects of the conceptual tools covered earlier in this chapter.

In an earlier era of social science, both physical-environmental and, more generally, spatial considerations were sequestered into geography as a specialist environmental and spatial discipline to consider; whereas temporal aspects were assigned to historians. Now, all social analysts must be prepared to address these aspects.

CONCLUSION

In this chapter, I have advanced a concept of a multi-dimensional approach to social structure. Several elements have to be assembled to understand the whole, and this chapter has laid out an extensive conceptual toolkit from which appropriate ideas can be drawn to accomplish particular types of analysis.

Chapter 6

CONCLUSIONS

In this final chapter, I consider the explanatory tasks social structural analysis is to perform. I then sketch out how the whole analytical apparatus advanced in this book – examined in principle and then in more detailed components – might be better integrated and put to work in order to engage in these tasks.

EXPLANATORY TASKS

One important way of conceptualising the task of social science is to see it as seeking to understand the patterns of behaviour and attitudes of people, especially their behaviour, since this can be empirically observed. This involves understanding the patterns in what people are and what they think, do and say. Sometimes, sociologists seem to limit this to a consideration of patterns of interaction among people, but this seems an unnecessarily limited focus, as important social action need not always involve (direct) contact with others. However, almost all social action arises in a broad context of interdependence (and often coordination) among people, whether or not they are actually present.

Although this might seem a reasonable end-goal for social explanation to achieve, it has several difficulties. One is that it assumes rather too continuous and smooth a flow of on-going human action, whereas there needs to be attention to the occasional (this varies empirically) discontinuities and breaks that severely upset apparently well-established patterns: e.g. revolutions. This difficulty might be overcome through maintaining a highly developed sensitivity to underlying tensions and mechanisms which shape longer-term structural developments, and to historically-important events.

Another difficulty is that this way of stating the problem does not adequately address the role of collective social entities. Rather, it tends to emphasise the importance of individuals located in the quite specific 'social situations' and flows of everyday life. Again, the difficulty can be overcome by extending the interest in patterns of attributes, attitudes and behaviour not just to individuals, but also to collective entities. So, the sociological issue becomes what and why people *and collective entities* think, do, interact, say etc. Or, put another way, the question being posed is: What is the range of social entities constituting a social structure, what is the pattern of their attributes and assets, and how are their behaviour and attitudes shaped?

However, even these reformulations are insufficient: explanation of these outcomes is but an intermediate step to a yet higher explanatory goal. Social structural explanation must also endeavour to show how the regular and also unusual patterns of allocations, behaviour and attitudes contribute to structural patterns of consistency and change in the on-going operation (and long-term tendencies) of social structures. After all, the detailed level of behaviour and attitudes has implicitly built into it wider consequences for the on-going operation of social structures or social formations as wholes. So it is not enough to examine the consequences of social structure: social structure itself must be looked at. This requires an understanding of the causal influence of various social units and actors on the overall trajectory of a social structure *itself* (its rise, maintenance, reformulations and eventual fall).

The problematics of social structural analysis can be further focused on a particular question (which I identified in Chapter 3 as being particularly posed by Durkheim). They concern the relationship between the 'division of labour' (how a social structure is organised, especially in terms of economic tasks) and the social integration of that social structure (how its members are welded into it). This concern is not only with the short-term operation of the social structure, but also with its longer-term trajectory: whether it is likely to blow up in a revolution, collapse into withdrawal, or merely plug along, largely unchanged, over a long period of time.

Social science understandings are limited, since they are seldom (if ever) deterministic, for a variety of reasons. Two important constraints on a 'natural science of society' are agency and historical contingency. In order to retain a focus on agency, it is important to keep the conception of social choices clearly at the forefront of any analysis. Social life is a continuous flow of decisions. In more specific form, this requires understanding of:

- the range of choices available to a person (or other social entity);
- the social processes involved with their decision-making; and
- the social constrains and resources available to them to undertake a particular option, rather than others which are foreclosed or not-preferred.

Actions and views will also be shaped by what has happened before, what other things are happening at the same time and what is happening elsewhere. New circumstances emerge, and yet experience and memory link us to the past. In the other direction, we partly shape our future by our expectations of it. These complexities require the social structural analyst to obtain some understanding of not only the objective constraints and opportunities involved for the people in a particular circumstance, but also how the constraints and opportunities are subjectively experienced. Again, both individuals and collective social actors need to be covered.

So, the explanatory task of social analysis is complex, covering both macro- and micro-levels, both the constants and the contingencies, and both subjective and objective aspects of social life.

ASSEMBLING THEORETICAL RESOURCES

Given this need for explanation, how can appropriate explanatory resources be assembled to tackle it? In reviewing the answers provided throughout this book, I shall first review a particular empirical way of handling this issue. I will then return to tentative lessons reviewed in the conclusion of Chapter 3, and then sketch out an approach that summarises much of the material I covered in Chapters 4 and 5.

One attempt to pull together several elements of social structural effects has been developed for empirical work in political sociology. (This mirrors similar work in other social research areas, but perhaps is somewhat more developed in this long-studied area.) This approach focuses on the patterns exhibited by people in relation to some particular institutionalised social choice. It then shows a way in which a wide range of social background variables might be assembled, drawing from several of the different areas covered in Chapter 5, and brought to bear on explaining these patterns of voting choice.

In the 'lifetime learning model' (Rose and MacAllister 1990), factors which might be expected to influence some social choice – e.g. voting – are organised into an ordered sequence of several 'blocks' each representing different stages of the life-cycle. (The methodological model is stepwise multiple-regression analysis, using blocks of variables.) The first block of variables involves social inheritance from parents (e.g. occupation of father and mother and their voting preferences). A further block centres on childhood and other socialisation experiences. The next block captures aspects of people's contemporary social backgrounds, and the final block focuses closely on immediate situational aspects (such as the effects of an election campaign). The usefulness of this framework is that it assembles into a single framework both contemporary and life-course considerations (together with some quite immediate situational influences). It can then arbitrate on which life-course stages, and which aspects of them, have direct or indirect influences on people's choices, and what the cumulative effect of all these influences is. In principle, it is easy enough to extend the framework used by Rose and McAllister by adding both network and organisational influences (as indicated by people's involvement in net- works and in organisations). (See Figure 6.1.) With these additions, it would be possible to string together a skeletal framework of influences on people's behaviour and attitudes, organised in a reasonable implied sequential order of where in the sequence their effect might be expected to 'kick in'.

This approach can further be extended by developing a similar summarising

128

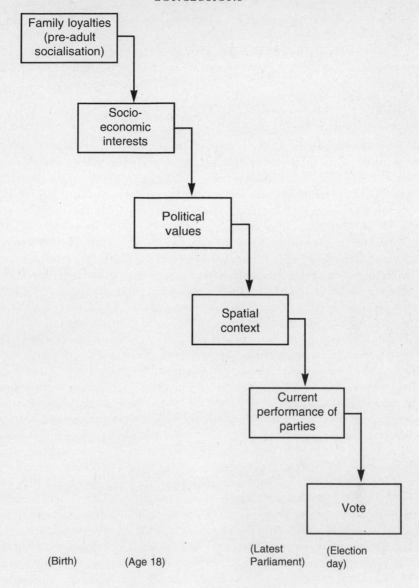

Figure 6.1 Diagram of lifetime learning model
Source: adapted from Rose and McAllister (1990)

framework for studying the effects on and from social collectivities. Much the same sets of causal frameworks could be worked up for each of the types of social entity that sociologists might be interested in. Then, further feedbacks and interactions between the analyses of different levels of units (collectivities and people) could be worked out.

But this whole language is too closely aligned to the requirements of empirical social research. Each of the variables in such lifetime learning and organisational models needs to be embedded within appropriate theoretical frameworks. Without adequate conceptualisation, stringing together a large sequence of variables may be instructive, but it will be quite *ad hoc*. However, especially if the several significant additions to the lifelong learning model were added in, it would be possible to anchor sophisticated theoretical discussions of complex social structural effects within an overall model suitable for research purposes. Certainly, there is some possibility of an empirical framework which would allow a more theoretically-based model of social structure to be empirically tested.

At a more technical level of data-analysis, there are, of course, more complex difficulties which render the operationalisation of this approach rather more difficult than I have indicated here, but the details of these technicalities are not immediately relevant. A major difficulty at the methods level is how to organise the multiplicity of variables involved. This is particularly so when apparently past effects may still also have a contemporary relevance: e.g. fathers' political preference may still be a contemporary influence on voting. Fortunately, techniques of data display such as path analysis can avoid the necessity of loading too much 'common variance' on particular variables by laying out chains of direct and indirect 'causality'.

However insightful and useful this model is, even in a considerably extended form it fails to deal with many issues I have raised throughout this book. Perhaps, though, it does point one way forward towards a more integrative approach.

A SUMMATIVE APPROACH

In this book, I have argued that there is a core at the heart of social structural analysis, although to study social structures in all their variability requires drawing on several of quite a range of conceptual frameworks. I have also argued that while the content of the ideas involved with any social structural analysis is important, this needs to be combined with appropriate views on how analysts should proceed, and their overall approach to sociology as a discipline.

The approach advocated here is to see sociology as providing a stock of concepts which are available to analyse particular social structures or groups of social structures. Sociologists need to be adept at using the various tools for structural analysis which this toolkit supplies, and the success or difficulties they experience should be reflected back to improve the toolkit of concepts. The central process of sociology is the dialectic of working between ideas and reality. Sensitivity to changing reality, together with continual improvement in the range of conceptual tools, should hopefully result in an ever-widening stock of insightful social analyses on the one hand and a better set of tools on the other.

But the assembly of stocks of studies and conceptual tools is not sufficient. Much theoretical work is needed to try to ensure that the various conceptual tools are welded together into more comprehensive frameworks and that their clashing assumptions and divergent perspectives are brought more into line with one another. A long theoretical and philosophical tradition in sociology can be drawn on in evaluating the success of particular conceptual tools in meeting the wider explanatory tasks sociology has long set itself. Continual theoretical tidying-up and innovation is needed.

In Chapter 2, a picture of the various 'fields of meaning' within which images of social structure can be developed was laid out. This was extended further in Chapter 4 where the agenda of theoretical issues which govern attempts to develop theoretically adequate social structural analyses was provided. It was shown that any account has to simultaneously meet often mutually-contradictory goals including:

- showing how micro-level interaction links up with macro-level collectivities;
- showing how subjective agency interrelates with objective structures;
- showing how social structures unfold over space and time.

It is doubtful if any one clearly consistent path can be followed through this maze of issues. It certainly is easier to map the overall maze of difficulties than to see a clear path through them.

At a more practical level, in Chapter 5 a range of conceptual tools to examine various of the dimensions of social structure was laid out. The conceptual resources needed include:

- classical status-and-role theory;
- network analyses;
- accounts of collective social actors;
- social constructionist accounts of the building and maintenance of social structures;
- distributional accounts of social structure;
- structural change analyses;
- life-course and life-event analyses; and
- spatial aspects of social structures.

It has been noted that sociologists often usefully communicate in short-hand by using the names of key writers as simulacra of wider positions associated with each name. So the names of key analysts can be used to eponymously indicate some of the major sources I draw upon in assembling my material on the various aspects of social structure. This is another way of summarising the material included in Chapter 5. In essence, I move from Merton (status-and role-sets) to Wellman and White *et al.* (networks), Coleman (collective actors), Bourdieu (social construction), Blau (social distributions), Marx (on resources) and to Oberschall and Zald (on social movement theory). Finally, I complement these with Elder, Riley *et al*. (life-courses), and Urry and others (on spatial and historical aspects). The combined ideas of these social theorists, complemented, of course, by extensions and critiques, constitute the central set of ideas needed to analyse social structure.

Any social structural analysis may require the use of various of these tools, and I consider that a full analysis would require them all.

The question of how these various tools relate to each other has hardly been dealt with. This requires much more argument than is possible here. Perhaps, as a quick way of summarising, the various types of tools can be related to three main types of task.

- Tools that assist in building up a picture of the social composition of a social order (social categories, networks, organisations etc.).
- Tools that assist in examining the various social processes involved in the production and reproduction of social structure (structure-building, peopling, researching etc.).
- Tools that examine the context in which social structures operate – especially the historical and spatial frameworks.

These three groups of perspectives correspond to broad types of model of social structure. The first relates to what I have termed an 'architectural model' and tends towards the building up of a static picture, whereas the second is a 'processural' model which tends to be quite dynamic. The third is a 'contextual' model which emphasises the arenas within which social structures operate. The temptation is to alternate between the first two approaches, starting off with the 'architectural' vision to retain a preliminary fix and then tracking the changes and processes using the 'processural' vision. However, the two can be melded together and a social structure seen as a sequence of points, phases or stages on a on-going path.

The 'architectural approach' (concerning the various layers of social units and their relationships) could have been tackled in several ways. In the rendition of Chapter 5, I employed a stratification of four levels, each a pair:

- individuals in their role and status-set settings; and then
- in their network contexts;
- organisations and similar less formal groupings; and then
- their contexts (e.g. the inter-organisational environment).

Within the 'processural' approach to analysing any social structure I drew attention in Chapter 5 to several main structural processes.

- *Social construction* Social structures are to some degree designed and also subject to maintenance, change and revolutionary processes, themselves at

132

least partially consciously-guided by people. This process produces (reproduces and changes) a set of 'boxes' or 'slots' together with the tasks assigned
each and an overall legitimacy for that structure.

- *Peopling* People are assigned to positions in the structure, and then operate
these positions (filled boxes) in ways that are required for that position,
together with other social considerations imported into that position by its
occupant.

- *Resourcing* Resources are generated by and also allocated among these
positions to ensure that the tasks can be carried out and to provide rewards
to members.

- *Social Control* People must be motivated by rewards and deterred from
undermining the overall structure by deviant behaviour.

- *Life-course* Whereby people move in structurally patterned ways through the
various positions in social structures.

- *System in operation (reproduction/change)* The structure then has to be put into
motion with the people both accommodating and also resisting and
reshaping the official social structure and creating an inhabited, on-going
and changing social structure. In this moment of analysis, the relationships
set up by the structure are seen to flower into action.

STEPS IN CARRYING OUT ANALYSES

Social analysis is not a static, dead thing: it should have a dynamic momentum
of its own. As analysts engage with different aspects of emergent social reality,
so too will their skills and stock of conceptual tools grow.

An important way of both summarising and concluding this book is to
return to my goal: i.e. that this book is designed in some part to rehearse how
social structures should be analysed. Let me suggest what the sequence of stages
in carrying out a social analysis of a particular social structure might be.

It should be helpful to consider several different tasks to which a social
structural analyst might aspire, ranging from quite simple description of an
aspect of a social structure, right through to a full-blown attempt to pull
together a theoretical model of how a social structure came into being and
the factors which shaped its course. Particular social structural analyses can
be classified into four main types: in terms of whether they are descriptive or
explanatory, and whether they are partial or complete. (Clearly, these are
somewhat arbitrary distinctions and much finer distinctions could be made.)
Associated with each of these alternative tasks is not just the size of the task,
but also the extent to which a full understanding of the social structure needs
to be explicitly developed. Partial descriptive accounts require the least
effort, whereas global explanatory analyses must reach much higher
standards.

Merton has depicted some of the tasks of the sociologist. Although he is
talking quite specifically about a sequence in the studies of roles, the general

point carries over into the wider study of social structures. He sees sociography as an essential descriptive base for then proceeding to a properly sociological explanatory level.

> It is possible to identify three types of accounts of roles: the depictive, the sociographic and the analytical. . . . The depictive accounts of social roles are representational portraits. The role of the business executive or the housewife or the labour leader is described in terms so concrete and vivid that the reader would at once recognise people engaged in these roles as soon as he met them. . . . Standing between the depictive, graphic art of the sociological novelist and the analytical, abstract formulation of the sociologist are the partly narrative, partly categorised descriptions of the sociographer. . . . The sociography of social roles narrates but does not place its principal characters in a more or less plot that helps the novelist exhibit a complexity of social relations. Sociography also classifies social roles but in categories drawn from everyday life rather than the more abstract formulations of sociological theory. . . . [These contain] fairly concrete descriptions of the norms embodied in a social role. . . . Beyond depiction and sociography, then, is the third way of examining social roles, the way of the sociological theorist. From the standpoint of theoretical sociology, social roles are combinations of designated properties and compounds of designated components.
>
> (Merton 1976: 12–14)

Merton's pithy evocation of the role of the structural analyst can be expanded. The following listing is rather more focused. It provides only some guidance about the main phases an analysis should go through. At several of these points any (and preferably several or maybe all) of the 11-point structural model described in Chapter 5 should be employed.

1 *Obtaining an experiential understanding* At the center of any social structural analysis you should be confident that you have obtained a good grasp of the operation of the social structure, preferably 'from the inside'. This is the well-known Weberian criterion of 'empathy' (sympathetic understanding'). Obviously, being a member of the social structure you are analysing (as is often the case with sociologists as opposed to anthropologists) is very helpful in providing a lived-in understanding. Another possibility is to be a temporary guest living within (or attached to) the social structure: e.g. in the capacity of a participant observer. If neither of these two classic research roles is possible, some alternative way of steeping yourself with appropriate experience is very important: e.g. reading material, talking with members or ex-members etc. It may be difficult to grasp what precisely is required to secure 'inside knowledge': essentially it means to have some experience of the routines and practices involved, of how people relate to each other, and of the limitations and opportunities

afforded by people's social positions. In Bourdieu's terms it would require a grasp of the 'habitus'. In Giddens's terms, this involves securing information about those practices conducted as an expression of the social structure.

2 *Checking the inside knowledge* However, the limitations imposed by this inside knowledge must also be guarded against. By the very nature of many social structures it will be partial and confined to particular parts of the social structure. Also, things may change across a variety of social circumstances (or even just over time). Consequently, it is important that steps be taken to ensure that personal and private experiences are checked against a wider range of people's experiences. Sometimes, this may require a research team where access to some corners of a social structure are denied researchers occupying certain roles (e.g. women's knowledge and experience may be difficult for male researchers to access). On occasions, too, systematic means may be required to ensure that a wide enough range of experience is being tapped (e.g. using surveys in large-scale and/or geographically-dispersed structures).

Obtaining a 'working understanding' of the practices within a social structure is a continuous guiding thread in building an analysis. It was not listed first because it is seen as a discrete exercise that can be 'knocked off' early on in the piece. It may rather be an understanding whose full significance dawns only as the investigation draws to a close. Rather, it was listed first because of its central and continuing importance.

On the other hand, it is not enough. As well as being mapped into only part of the overall social structure, inside knowledge may lead to 'psychologising'. In 'folk knowledge' employing 'native theories', things are often seen from the view of individuals and are often personalised. But this does not mean that the analysis should remain trapped at this level. Rather, a good social structural analysis will build on the experiential core in order to understand the social dimensions of the situation.

3 *Setting boundaries/providing definitions* A knotty issue that must be faced up to at some point in the study is coming to some decision about the boundaries of the structure, providing a general definition of it, or even a name for it. There may also be components or particular sub-structures that may operate in quite different ways that need to be demarcated within the analysis. There is no obvious place where this particular task can be 'correctly' inserted into the sequence of an analysis. Clearly, a preliminary attempt is required early on (how else can some sense be obtained of what might or might not be relevant?). But a more refined grasp of critical boundaries will only be established as the analysis proceeds. (And hopefully any appallingly bad early decision can be rectified without penalty.)

4 *Description of components* An important preparatory step in an investigation is to conduct a 'role inventory'. This involves a listing of the range of roles that are available and, for each, what expectations are held of its

occupants, and what resources are usually assigned them. This includes the properties of collective entities as well.

5 *Status systems*   Clearly, a role inventory covers only the bare bones of the social structure and remains at a descriptive level. The next task is to assemble the picture of how the different roles relate to each other, so that the various structural patterns can be shown at work. Such assemblages might include inter-related roles such as a family composed of mother/wife, father/husband and children/siblings. It is important to show exactly how these role-clusters actually *inter-relate* (e.g. the ways expectations, resources, social control etc. are involved with their operation).

6 *Internal relations*   The next major step is to sweep up the understanding of the various role-clusters into a wider understanding of the whole social structure. At this level, specification is required of the way each role-cluster relates to all others in the structure, and also any internal logic the structure as a whole may have, above and beyond that involved with the various relationships among its role-clusters.

   At this point I would like to suggest, in summary, a 'guiding thread' for carrying out analyses (see also the sketch of the nature of social structures provided in Chapter 4). Social structure involves, above all, the ways in which social groupings are involved in (strategies and tactics) drawing on and creating ideologies, resources and contacts to maintain and/or change their position within the broad social order. But their abilities to carry out such 'projects' will vary considerably.

7 *Structural change*   The penultimate step is to reach beyond the static understanding of a social structure at a particular point in time and space and to be able to specify the social conditions which affect its rise, continuance and decline, and also to be able to model its internal logic and its likely trajectory.

8 *Host verification*   The final step always pertains, whatever the level of completeness and explanatory fullness that has been achieved. This is to return to the core experience of the inside knowledge about the social structure and to check that the models that have been developed are compatible with the lived experience of people in the social structure. A more specific format for carrying out this step is 'host verification' where the researcher goes back to his/her subjects with their findings to attempt to validate their study from the viewpoint of the participants. Again, this is a complex step since participants may incorrectly deny an account which has been put forward.

ENVOIE

This book has enjoined a goal and justification for studying social structures, and discussed various issues which are relevant to their analysis. It has provided much resource material in the form of summaries of ideas for analysing social structures, together with references to other sources where these ideas might be considered at far greater length. It has identified many gaps in our existing knowledge of social structures which deserve greater attention. However, the point of being a sociologist is not just to study what others have written. This book has, above all, been concerned with encouraging and assisting in the craft of analysing particular social structures in order to build up more general understanding of social structures. It is hoped that the reader will press into practice the material covered in this book.

BIBLIOGRAPHY

Abercrombie, N., Hill, S. and Turner, B. (1980) *The Dominant Ideology Thesis*, London: Allen & Unwin.

Abrams, P. (1982) *Historical Sociology*, Somerset: Open Books.

Ahrne, G. (1994) *Social Organisations: Interaction Inside, Outside and between Organisations*, London: Sage.

Aldrich, H. and Marsden, P. (1988) 'Environments and organizations' in N. Smelser (ed.) *Handbook of Sociology*, Newbury Park: Sage, 361–92.

Alexander, J. (1984) 'Social-structural analysis: some notes on its history and prospects' *Sociological Quarterly*, 25 (1), 5–26.

Alexander, J. (ed.) (1985) *Neo-Functionalism*, Beverly Hills: Sage.

—— (1987) *The Micro–Macro Link*, Berkeley: University of California Press.

Anderson, B. (1983) *Imagined Communities*, London: Verso.

Andrews, H. (1993) 'Durkheim and social morphology' in S. Turner (ed.) *Emile Durkheim: Sociologist and Moralist*, London: Routledge.

Archer, M. (1982) 'Structuration versus morphogenesis: on combining structure and action' *British Journal of Sociology*, 33 (4), 445–83.

—— (1988) *Culture and Agency: the Place of Culture in Social Theory*, Cambridge: Cambridge University Press.

—— (1995) *Realist Social Theory: the Morphogenetic Approach*, Cambridge: Cambridge University Press.

Baudrilliard, J. (1983) *In the Shadow of the Silent Majorities or the End of the Social*, New York: Semiotext.

Bauman, Z. (1990) *Thinking Sociologically*, Oxford: Blackwell.

Becker, H. (1970) *Sociological Work*, Chicago: Aldine.

Ben-David, J. (1971) *The Role of the Scientist in Society*, New Jersey: Prentice Hall (Second edn., 1984)

Berger, P. and Luckmann, T. (1966) *The Social Construction of Social Reality*, Harmondsworth: Penguin.

Bhaskar, R. (1979) *The Possibility of Naturalism: a Philosophical Critique of the Contemporary Human Sciences*, Atlantic Heights: Humanities Press.

Biddle, B. (1987) 'Recent developments in role theory' *Annual Review of Sociology*, 12, 67–92.

Blalock, H. (1990) *Understanding Social Inequality: Processes of Allocation*, California: Sage.

Blau, J. (1993) *Social Contracts and Economic Markets*, New York: Plenum Press.

Blau, P. (ed.) (1975) *Approaches to the Study of Social Structure*, New York: Free Press.

Blau, P. (1977) *Inequality and Heterogeneity: a Primitive Theory of Social Structure*, New York: Free Press.

138

—— (1994) *Structural Contexts of Opportunities*, Chicago: University of Chicago Press.

Blau, P. and Duncan, O. D. (1967) *The American Occupational Structure*, New York: Wiley.

Blau, P. and Merton, R. K. (eds.) (1981) *Continuities in Structural Inquiry*, Beverly Hills: Sage.

Blau, P. and Schwartz, J. (1984) *Crosscutting Social Circles*, Orlando: Academic Press.

Block, F. (1990) *Postindustrial Possibilities: a Critique of Economic Discourse*, California: University of California Press.

Bogard, W. (1990) 'Closing down the social: Baudrillard's challenge to contemporary sociology' *Sociological Theory*, 8 (1), 1–15.

Boltanski, L. (1987 [1982]) *The Making of a Class: Cadres in French Society*, Cambridge: Cambridge University Press.

Bott, E. (1957) *Family and Social Network*, London: Tavistock.

Bourdieu, P. and Wacquant, L. J. D (1992) *An Invitation to Reflexive Sociology*, Cambridge: Polity Press.

Buechler, S. (1993) 'Beyond resource mobilization? Emerging trends in social movement theory' *Sociological Quarterly*, 34 (2), 217–35.

Burns, T. and Flam, H. (1987) *The Shaping of Social Organisation: Social Rule Theory with Applications*, California: Sage.

Burt, R. S. (1987) 'Social contagion and innovation: cohesion versus structural equivalence' *American Journal of Sociology*, 92 (6), 1287–335.

—— (1992) *Structural Holes: the Social Structure of Competition*, Massachusetts: Harvard University Press.

Calhoun, C., LiPuma, E. and Postone, M. (eds) (1993) *Bourdieu: Critical Perspectives*, Cambridge: Polity Press.

Calhoun, C., Meyer, M. and Scott, W. R. (eds) (1990) *Structures of Power and Constraint: Papers in Honor of Peter Blau*, Cambridge: Cambridge University Press.

Callinicos, A. (1987) *Making History: Agency, Structure and Change in Social Theory*, Cambridge: Polity Press.

—— (1989) *Against Postmodernism: a Marxist Critique*, Cambridge: Polity Press.

Castoriadis, C. (1987 [1975]) *The Imaginary Institution of Society*, Cambridge: Polity Press (trans. K. Blamey).

Clagett, A. (1988) 'Theoretical consideration of integrating social structure into symbolic interactionism: selected methodological insights' *Social Behaviour and Personality*, 16 (1), 97–108.

Clark, J. (ed) (1990) *Anthony Giddens: Consensus and Controversy*, Hants: Falmer Press.

Cohen, A., Adoni, H. and Bantz, C. (1990) *Social Conflict and Television News*, California: Sage.

Cohen, G. (ed.) (1987) *Social Change and the Life Course*, London: Routledge.

Cohen, P. (1968) *Modern Social Theory*, London: Heinneman.

Cole, S. (1979) *The Sociological Orientation*, Chicago: Rand McNally.

Coleman, J. (1982) *The Asymmetrical Society*, Syracuse: Syracuse University Press.

—— (1990) *Foundations of Social Theory*, Massachusetts: Harvard University Press.

Connell, B. (1983 [1979]) 'The concept of role and what to do with it' in B. Connell (ed.) *Which Way is Up?*, Sydney: George Allen & Unwin, 189–207.

Cook, K. S. and Whittmeyer, J. M. (1992) 'Two approaches to social structure: exchange theory and network analysis' *Annual Review of Sociology*, 18, 109–27.

Coser, L. (ed.) (1975) *The Idea of Social Structure: Papers in Honor of Robert K Merton*, New York: Harcourt, Brace & Jovanovich.

Coser, R. (1960) 'Laughter among colleagues' *Psychiatry*, 23, 81–95.

—— (1991) *In Defense of Modernity: Role Complexity and Individual Autonomy*, Stanford: Stanford University Press.

Crothers, C. (1987) *Robert K Merton*, London: Routledge.
—— (1991) 'The internal structure of sociology departments: the role of graduate students and others groups' *Teaching Sociology*, 19 (3), 333–43.
Dahrendorf, R. (1968) *Essays in the Theory of Society*, London: Routledge & Kegan Paul.
Denzin, N. (1992) *Symbolic Interactionism and Cultural Studies*, Oxford: Blackwell.
Dex, S. (ed.) (1991) *Life and Work History Analyses: Qualitative and Quantitative Developments*, London: Routledge.
DiPretto, T. and Forristal, A. (1994) 'Multilevel models: methods and substance' *Annual Review of Sociology*, 20, 331–57.
Donzelot, J. (1988) 'The promotion of the social' *Economy and Society*, 17 (3), 73–84.
Duncan, O. D. and Schnore, L. (1959) 'Cultural, behavioral and ecological perspectives in the study of social organisation' *American Journal of Sociology*, 65, 132–46.
Durkheim, E. (1893 [1947]) *The Division of Labour in Society*, New York: Free Press.
—— (1952) *Suicide: a Study in Sociology*, London: Routledge & Kegan Paul.
Eisenstadt, S. and Helle, H. (eds) (1985) *Macro-Sociological Theory: Perspectives on Sociological Theory*, London: Sage.
Eister, A. (1964) 'Social structure' in J. Gold (ed.) *A Dictionary of the Social Sciences*, London: Tavistock, 668–9.
Elder, G. (1994) 'Time, human agency, and social change: perspectives on the life course' *Social Psychology Quarterly*, 57 (1), 4–15.
Elias, N. (1978) *What is Sociology?*, London: Hutchinson.
Emirbayer, M. and Goodwin, J. (1994) 'Network analysis, culture and the problem of agency' *American Journal of Sociology*, 99 (6), 1411–54.
Etzioni, A. (1964) *Modern Organisations*, Englewood Heights: Prentice Hall.
—— (1968) *The Active Society*, New York: Free Press.
Fielding, N. (ed.) (1988) *Actions and Structures*, London: Sage.
Firth, R. (1951) *Elements of Social Organization*, London: Watts.
—— (1964) *Essays on Social Organization and Values*, London: Athlone Press (LSE Monographs on Social Anthropology 28).
Foran, J. (1993) 'Theories of revolution revisited: toward a fourth generation?' *Sociological Theory*, 11 (1), 1–20.
Fuchs, S. (1989) 'On the micro-foundations of macrosociology: a critique of microsociological reductionism' *Sociological Perspectives*, 32, 169–82.
Gallie, W. B. (1956 [1955]) 'Essentially contested concepts' *Proceedings of the Aristotelean Society*, 46, 167–98.
Gans, H. (1968) *People and Plans*, New York: Basic Books.
Garnsey, E. (1981) 'The rediscovery of the division of labour' *Theory and Society*, 10, 325–36.
Gellner, E. (1973) *Cause and Meaning in the Social Sciences*, London: Routledge & Kegan Paul.
—— (1985) *Relativism and the Social Sciences*, Cambridge: Cambridge University Press.
George, L. (1993) 'Sociological perspectives on life transitions' *Annual Review of Sociology*, 19, 353–73.
Giddens, A. (1960) 'Aspects of the social structure of a university hall of residence' *Sociological Review*, 8, 97–108.
—— (1979) *Central Problems in Social Theory: Action, Structure and Contradiction in Social Analysis*, London: Macmillan.
—— (1984) *The Constitution of Society*, Oxford: Polity Press.
Gilbert, M. (1989) *On Social Facts*, London: Routledge.
Glucksmann, M. (1974) *Structuralist Analysis in Contemporary Social Thought*, London: Routledge & Kegan Paul.

Gould, M. (1987) *Revolution in the Development of Capitalism: the Coming of the English Revolution*, Berkley: University of California Press.

Granovetter, M. (1973) 'The strength of weak ties' *American Journal of Sociology*, 78 (6), 1360–80.

—— (1979) 'The theory-gap in social network analysis' in P. Holland and S. Leinhardt (eds) *Perspectives in Social Network Research*, New York: Academic Press.

—— (1983) 'The strength of weak ties: a network theory revisited' *Sociological Theory*, 1, 201–33.

—— (1988) Preface in Wellman and Berkowitz (1988).

Granovetter, M. and Swedberg, R. (eds) (1992) *The Sociology of Economic Life*, Boulder: Westview Press.

Gurnah, A. and Scott, A. (1992) *The Uncertain Science: Criticisms of Sociological Formalism*, London: Routledge.

Hall, P. (1987) 'Interactionism and the study of social organisation' *Sociological Quarterly*, 28, 1–22.

Handel, W. (1979) 'normative expectations and emergence of meaning as solutions to problems: convergence of structural and interactionist views' *American Journal of Sociology*, 84 (4), 855–81.

Haugaard, M. (1992) *Structures, Restructuration and Social Power*, Aldershot: Avebury.

Hays, S. (1994) 'Structure and agency and the sticky problem of culture' *Sociological Theory*, 12 (1), 57–72.

Hechter, M. (ed.) (1990) *Social Institutions: their Emergence, Maintenance and Effects*, New York: Aldine.

Heer, D. (1992) 'Social structure' in W. Outwaite and T. Bottomore (comps.) *Blackwell Dictionary of Twentieth Century Social Thought*, Cambridge: Blackwell.

Helle, H. J. and Eisenstadt, S. N. (eds) (1985) *Microsociological Theory: Perspectives on Sociological Theory*, California: Sage.

Hilbert, J (1981) 'Toward an improved understanding of role theory and society' *Theory and Society*, 10 (2), 207–26.

Hindess, B. (1989) *Political Choice and Social Structure: an Analysis of Actors, Interests and Rationality*, Aldershot: Edward Elgar.

Holmwood, J. and Stewart, A. (1991) *Explanation and Social Theory*, London: Macmillan.

Hopkins, T. and Wallerstein, I. (1982) *World-Systems Analysis: Theory and Methodology*, Beverly Hills: Sage.

Huber, J. (ed.) (1991) *Macro–Micro Linkages in Sociology*, California: Sage.

Jackson, E. F. and Curtis, R. F. (1972) 'Effects of verticial mobility and status inconsistency: a body of negative evidence' *American Sociological Review*, 37, 701–13.

Jenkins, C. (1983) 'Resource mobilisation and the study of social movements' *Annual Review of Sociology*, 9, 527–53.

Keat, N. and Urry, J. (1975) *Social Theory as Science*, London: Routledge & Kegan Paul.

Knorr-Cetina, K. and Cicourel, A. V. (eds) (1981) *Advances in Social Theory and Methodology: Toward an Integration of Micro- and Macro-Sociologies*, Boston: Routledge & Kegan Paul.

Knottnerus, J. D. and Prendergast, C. (eds) (1994) *Recent Developments in the Theory of Social Structure*, Greenwich, Conneticut: JAI Press.

Kohn, M. (1989) 'Social structure and personality: a quintissentially sociological approach to social psychology' *Social Forces*, 68 (1), 26–33.

Kontopoulos, K. (1993) *The Logics of Social Structure*, Cambridge: Cambridge University Press.

Kroeber, A. L. and Parsons, T. (1958) 'The concepts of culture and of social system' *American Sociological Review*, 23, 582–3.

Kuhn, M. (1960) 'Self-attitudes by age, sex and professional training' *Sociological Quarterly*, 1, 39–55.

Kuper, A. (1983) *Anthropology and Anthropologists: the Modern British School*, (revised edn) London: Routledge & Kegan Paul.

Lash, S. (ed.) (1990) *The Sociology of Post-Modernism*, London: Routledge.

Lash, S. and Urry, J. (1984) 'The new Marxism of collective action: a critical analysis' *Sociology*, 18 (1), 33–50.

Layder, D. (1990) *The Realist Image in Social Science*, New York: St Martin's Press.

—— (1994) *Understanding Social Theory*, London: Sage.

Lazarsfeld, P. F. and Menzel, H. (1961) 'On the relation between individual and collective properties' in A. Etzioni (ed.) *A Sociological Reader in Complex Organizations*, New York: Holt, Rinehart & Winston, 499–516.

Leach, E. (1968) 'Social structure: the history of the concept' in D. Sills (ed.) *International Encyclopedia of the Social Sciences*, New York: Macmillan, 482–9.

Lenski, G. (1954) 'Status crystallization: a nonvertical dimension of social status' *American Sociological Review*, 19, 405–13.

Lévi-Strauss, C. (1952) 'Social structure' in A. L. Kroeber (ed.) *Anthropology Today*, Chicago: University of Chicago Press, 524–53.

—— (1963) *Structural Anthropology*, New York: Basic Books.

Lipset, S. M. (1963) *Political Man: the Social Basis of Politics*, New York: Doubleday Anchor.

Lloyd, C. (1993) *The Structures of History*, Oxford: Blackwell.

Lockwood, D. (1992) *Solidarity and Schism: 'the Problem of Disorder' in Durkheimian and Marxist sociology*, Oxford: Clarendon Press.

Lowie, R. (1932) 'Social organisation' in E. Seligman and A. Johnson (eds) *Encyclopedia of Social Science*, 14, New York: Macmillan, 141–9.

Macpherson, C. and Macpherson, L. (1987) 'Towards an explanation of recent trends in suicide in Western Samoa' *Man*, 22, 305–30.

Maines, D. (ed) (1991) *Social Organization and Social Process: Essays in Honor of Anselm Strauss*, New York: Aldine de Gruyter.

Manicas, P. (1987) *The History and Philosophy of the Social Sciences*, Oxford: Basic Books.

Marx, K. (1913 [1852]) *The Eighteenth Brumaire of Louis Bonaparte*, New York: International Publishers.

—— (1959) 'Preface to the critique of Political Economy' in *Early Writings* :McGraw Hill.

—— (1971 [1882]) *Capital: a Critque of Political Economy*, London: Penguin.

Mayer, A. (1966) 'The significance of quasi-groups in the study of complex societies' in M. Banton (ed.) *The Social Anthropology of Complex Societies*, London: Tavistock.

Mayhew, B. (1980/81) 'Structuralism v. individualism' *Social Forces*, 59, 335–75, 627–48.

Mennell, S. (1983) 'Social structure' in M. Mann (ed.) *Dictionary of Sociology*, London: Macmillan, 362.

Merton, R. K. (1968 [1949]) *Social Theory and Social Structure*, Glencoe, Illinois: Free Press.

—— (1976) *Sociological Ambivalence*, New York: Free Press.

Meyer, M. (1990) 'The Weberian tradition in organizational research' in Calhoun *et al.* (1990): 191–216.

Mills, C. W. (1959) *The Sociological Imagination*, London: Penguin.

—— (ed) (1960) *Images of Man: the Classical Tradition in Sociological Thinking*, New York: Braziller.

Morris, A. and Mueller, C. (eds) (1992) *Frontiers in Social Movement Theory*, New Haven: Yale University Press.

Mouzelis, N. (1990) *Post-Marxist Alternatives: the Construction of Social Orders*, London: Macmillan.
—— (1991) *Back to Sociological Theory: the Construction of Social Orders*, London: Macmillan.
—— (1993) 'On figurational sociology' *Theory, Culture and Society*, 10, 239–53.
—— (1995) *Sociological Theory: What Went Wrong?*, London: Routledge.
Mulkay, M. (1988) *On Humour: Its Nature and Its Place in Modern Society*, Cambridge: Polity Press.
Mullins, N. (1973) *Theories and Theory-Groups in Contemporary American Sociology*, New York: Holt, Rinehart & Winston.
Murdock, G. (1949) *Social Structure*, New York: Macmillan.
Murphy, R. (1988) *Social Closure: the Theory of Monopolization*, Oxford: Oxford University Press.
Murphy, R. F. (1972) *The Dialectics of Social Life*, London: George Allen & Unwin.
Nadel, S. F. (1957) *The Theory of Social Structure*, Melbourne: Melbourne University Press.
Namboordi, K. and Corwin, R. (1993) *The Logic and Method of Sociology: an Input–Output approach to Organizational Networks*, Westport, Connecticut: Praeger.
Nohria, N. and Eccles, R. G. (eds) (1992) *Networks and Organisations: Structure, Form and Action*, Boston: Harvard Business School Press.
O'Rand, A. and Krecker, M. (1990) 'Concepts of the life cycle: their history, meanings and uses in the social sciences' *Annual Review of Sociology*, 16, 241–62.
Ogles, R., Levy, M. and Parsons, T. (1959) 'Culture and social system: an exchange' *American Sociological Review*, 24, 246–50.
Parsons, T. (1973) 'Culture and social structure revisited' in L. Schneider and C. Bonjean (eds) *The Idea of Culture in the Social Sciences*, Cambridge: Cambridge University Press.
Parsons, T. and Shils, E. (eds) (1951) *Toward a General Theory of Action*, Harvard: Harvard University Press.
Perrow, C. (1970) *Organisational Analysis: a Sociological View*, London: Tavistock.
Porpora, D. (1987) *The Concept of Social Structure*, Westport, Conneticut: Greenwood Press.
—— (1989) 'Four concepts of social structure' *Journal for the Theory of Social Behaviour*, 19 (2), 195–212.
—— (1993) 'Cultural rules and material relations' *Sociological Theory*, 11 (2), 212–29.
Radcliffe-Brown, A. R. (1957 [1948]) *A Natural Science of Society*, Glencoe, Illinois: Free Press.
Reed, M. and Hughes, M. (1992) *Rethinking Organisations: New Directions in Organisation Theory and Analysis*, London: Sage.
Ridgeway, C. (ed.) (1994) 'Conceptualising structure in social psychology' *Social Psychology Quarterly*, (special issue) 57.
Ritzer, G. (1991) *Metatheorizing in Sociology*, Lexington, Massachusetts: Lexington Books.
Rose, R. and MacAllister, I. (1990) *The Loyalties of Voters: a Lifetime Learning Model*, London: Sage.
Rubenstein, D. (1992) 'Structural explanation in sociology: the egalitarian imperative' *American Sociologist*, 23 (2), 5–19.
Runciman, W. G. (1989) *A Treatise on Social Theory*, Cambridge: Cambridge University Press.
Sayer, A. (1991 [1984]) *Method in Social Science: a Realist Approach*, London: Routledge (2nd edn.).

BIBLIOGRAPHY

Sayer, A. and Walker, R. (1992) *The New Social Economy: Reworking the Division of Labour*, Cambridge, Massachusetts: Blackwell.

Scott, J. (1991) *Social Network Analysis: a Handbook*, London: Sage.

Scott, R. (1993) 'Recent developments in organizational sociology' *Acta Sociologica*, 36, 63–8.

Sewell, W. H. Jr. (1992) 'A theory of structure: duality, agency and transformation' *American Journal of Sociology*, 98 (1), 1–29.

Short, J. (ed.) (1986) *The Social Fabric*, California: Sage.

Sills, D. and Merton, R. K. (eds) (1991) *Social science quotations, International Encyclopedia of Social Sciences, Vol. 19*, New York: Macmillan.

Skocpol, T (1979) *States and Revolutions*, Cambridge: Cambridge University Press.

—— (ed.) (1984) *Vision and Method in Historical Sociology*, Cambridge: Cambridge University Press.

Smart, B. (1990) 'On the disorder of things: sociology, postmodernity and the "end of the social" ' *Sociology*, 24 (3), 397–416.

Smelser, N. (1988) 'Social structure' in N. Smelser (ed.) *Handbook of Sociology*, Newbury Park: Sage, 103–29.

Stinchcombe, A. (1968) *Constructing Social Theories*, New York: Harcourt, Brace & World.

—— (1975) 'Merton's theory of social structure' in Coser (ed.) *The Idea of Social Structure*, New York: Harcourt, Brace, Jovanovich, 11–34.

—— (1983) *Economic Sociology*, New York: Academic Press.

Stone, K. (1974) 'The origins of job structures in the steel industry' *Review of Radical Political Economics*, 6 (2), 113–73.

Storer, N. (1966) *The Social System of Science*, New York: Harcourt, Rinehart & Winston.

Sztompka, P. (1991) *Society in Action: a Theory of Social Becoming*, Cambridge: Polity Press.

Tiger, L. and Fox, R. (1971) *The Imperial Animal*, London: Secker & Warburg.

Tilly, C. (1981) *As Sociology Meets History*, New York: Academic Press.

—— (1984) *Big Structures, Large Processes, Huge Comparisons*, New York: Russell Sage Foundation.

Turner, J. (1992) 'The production and reproduction of social solidarity: a synthesis of two rational choice theories' *Journal for the Theory of Social Behaviour*, 22 (3), 311–28.

Turner, J. and Beeghley, L. (1981) *The Emergence of Sociological Theory*, Homewood, Illinois: Dorsey Press.

Udy, S. H. (1968) 'Social structure: social structural analysis' in D. Sills (ed.) *International Encyclopedia of Social Sciences, 14*, New York: Macmillan.

Veiel, H. and Baumann, U. (1992) (eds.) *The Meaning and Measurement of Social Support*, New York: Hemisphere.

Warner, W. L. (1967) *The Emergent American Society: Large Scale Organisations*, New Haven: Yale University Press.

Weber, M. (1947) *The Theory of Social and Economic Organisation*, Glencoe, Illinois: Free Press.

Wellman, B. and Berkowitz, S. D. (eds) (1988) *Social Structures: a Network Approach*, New York: Cambridge University Press.

White, H. (1992) *Identity and Control: a Structural Theory of Social Action*, Princeton: Princeton University Press.

White, M. R. (1973) 'Aging and cohort succession: interpretations and misrepresentations' *Public Opinion Quarterly*, 37, 35–49.

Whitt, H. (1983) 'Status inconsistency: a body of negative evidence or a statistical artifact?' *Social Forces*, 62 (1), 201–33.

144

BIBLIOGRAPHY

Williams, R. (1983) *Keywords: a Vocabulary of Culture and Society*, Oxford: Oxford University Press.

Wilson, J. (1983) *Social Theory*, New Jersey: Prentice Hall.

Wright, E. (ed.) (1989) *The Debate on Classes*, Verso: London.

Wrong, D. (1961) 'The oversocialised conception of man in modern society' *American Sociological Review*, 26, 187–93.

INDEX